Educ Dev
PA
30
ol

LIFE HISTORY RESEARCH IN
EDUCATIONAL SETTINGS

DOING QUALITATIVE RESEARCH IN EDUCATIONAL SETTINGS

Series Editor: Pat Sikes

The aim of this series is to provide a range of high quality introductory research methods texts. Each volume focuses, critically, on one particular methodology enabling a detailed yet accessible discussion. All of the contributing authors are established researchers with substantial practical experience. While every book has its own unique style, each discusses the historical background of the approach, epistemological issues and appropriate uses. They then go on to describe the operationalization of the approach in educational settings drawing upon specific and vivid examples from the authors' own work. The intention is that readers should come away with a level of understanding that enables them to feel sufficiently confident to undertake their own research as well as to critically evaluate other accounts of research using the approach.

Published and forthcoming titles

Michael Bassey: *Case Study Research in Educational Settings*
Peter Clough: *Narratives and Fictions in Educational Research*
Ivor Goodson and Pat Sikes: *Life History Research in Educational Settings*
Morwenna Griffiths: *Educational Research for Social Justice*
Gary McCulloch and William Richardson: *Historical Research in Educational Settings*
Jenny Ozga: *Policy Research in Educational Settings*
Christopher Pole and Marlene Morrison: *Ethnography in Educational Settings*
Hilary Radnor: *Researching Your Professional Practice*

LIFE HISTORY RESEARCH IN EDUCATIONAL SETTINGS

Learning from lives

Ivor F. Goodson and Pat Sikes

Open University Press
Buckingham · Philadelphia

Open University Press
Celtic Court
22 Ballmoor
Buckingham
MK18 1XW

email: enquiries@openup.co.uk
world wide web: www.openup.co.uk

and
325 Chestnut Street
Philadelphia, PA 19106, USA

First Published 2001

A catalogue record of this book is available from the British Library

ISBN   0 335 20713 8 (pb)   0 335 20714 6 (hb)

Library of Congress Cataloging-in-Publication Data
Goodson, Ivor.
    Life history research in educational settings: learning from lives/Ivor F. Goodson
and Pat Sikes.
        p.   cm. – (Doing qualitative research in educational settings)
    Includes bibliographical references and index.
    ISBN 0-335-20714-6 – ISBN 0-335-20713-8 (pbk.)
    1. Biography–Research–Methodology.   2. Biography as a literary form–Study
and teaching. I. Sikes, Patricia J.   II. Title.   III. Series.
CT22.G66 2001
808'.06692–dc21   2001021070

Typeset by Type Study, Scarborough
Printed in Great Britain by St Edmundsbury Press Ltd, Bury St Edmunds, Suffolk

The struggle of people against power is
the struggle of memory against forgetting.

Milan Kundera

Contents

Series editor's preface

I had never realized just how fascinating research was in its own right. I was expecting the research methods course to be boring, difficult and all about statistics but I couldn't have been more wrong. There is so much to consider, so many aspects, so many ways of finding out what's going on, and not just one way of representing it too. I have been really surprised.

(Student taking an MA in Educational Studies)

I never knew that there was so much to research. I thought that you just chose a method, applied it, did your statistical sums and came up with your findings. The reality is more complicated but so much more interesting and meaningful.

(Student taking an MA in Educational Studies)

The best thing for me was being told that qualitative research is 'proper' research – providing it's done properly of course. What goes on in schools is so complex and involves so many different perspectives that I think you often need a qualitative approach to begin to get some idea of what's going on.

(Student taking an MA in Sociology)

I really appreciate hearing about other researcher's experiences of doing research. It was quite a revelation when I first became aware that things don't always go as smoothly as some written accounts seem to suggest. It's really reassuring to hear honest reports: they alert you to pitfalls and problems and things that you might not have thought about.

(Doctoral student)

Comments such as these will be familiar to anyone who has ever taught or taken a course which aims to introduce the range of research approaches available to social scientists in general and those working in educational settings in particular.

The central message that they convey seems to be that the influence of the positivist scientist paradigm is both strong and pervasive, shaping expectations of what constitutes 'proper', 'valid' and 'worthwhile' research. What Barry Troyna wrote in 1994, continues to be the case; namely that:

> There is a view which is already entrenched and circulating widely in the populist circles ... that qualitative research is subjective, value-laden and, therefore, unscientific and invalid, in contrast to quantitative research, which meets the criteria of being objective, value-free, scientific and therefore valid.
>
> (1994: 9)

Within academic and research circles though, where the development of post-modernist and post-structuralist ideas have affected both thinking and research practice, it can be easy to forget what the popular perspective is. This is because, in these communities, qualitative researchers from the range of theoretical standpoints, utilize a variety of methods, approaches, strategies and techniques in the full confidence that their work is rigorous, legitimate and totally justifiable as research. And the process of peer review serves to confirm that confidence.

Recently, however, for those concerned with and involved in research in educational settings, and especially for those engaged in educational research, it seems that the positivist model, using experimental, scientific, quantitative methods, is definitely in the ascendancy once again. Those of us working in England and Wales, go into the new millennium with the government endorsed exhortation to produce evidence-based research which,

> (firstly) demonstrates conclusively that if teachers change their practice from x to y there will be significant and enduring improvement in teaching and learning; and (secondly) has developed an effective method of convincing teachers of the benefits of, and means to, changing from x to y.
>
> (Hargreaves 1996: 5)

If it is to realize its commendable aims of school effectiveness and school improvement, research as portrayed here, demands 'objectivity', experiments and statistical proofs. There is a problem with this requirement though and the essence of it is that educational institutions and the individuals who are involved in and with them are a heterogeneous bunch with different attributes, abilities, aptitudes, aims, values, perspectives, needs and so on. Furthermore these institutions and individuals are located within complex social contexts with all the implications and influences that this entails. On its own, research whose findings can be expressed in mathematical terms is unlikely to be sophisticated enough to sufficiently accommodate and account for the myriad differences that are involved. As one group of prominent educational researchers have noted:

We will argue that schooling does have its troubles. However, we maintain that the analysis of the nature and location of these troubles by
the school effectiveness research literature, and in turn those writing
Department for Employment and Education policy off the back of this
research, is oversimplified, misleading and thereby educationally and
politically dangerous (notwithstanding claims of honourable intent).

(Slee *et al.* 1998: 2–3)

There is a need for rigorous research which does not ignore, but rather
addresses, the complexity of the various aspects of schools and schooling:
for research which explores and takes account of different objective experiences and subjective perspectives, and which acknowledges that qualitative
information is essential, both in its own right and also in order to make full
and proper use of quantitative indicators. The Doing Qualitative Research
in Educational Settings series of books is based on this fundamental belief.
Thus the overall aims of the series are: to illustrate the potential that particular qualitative approaches have for research in educational settings, and
to consider some of the practicalities involved and issues that are raised
when doing qualitative research so that readers will feel equipped to embark
on research of their own.

At this point it is worth noting that qualitative research is difficult to
define as it means different things at different times and in different contexts.
Having said this Denzin and Lincoln's (1994) generic definition offers a
useful starting point:

Qualitative research is multimethod in focus, involving an interpretive,
naturalistic approach to its subject matter. This means that qualitative
researchers study things in their natural settings, attempting to make sense
of, or interpret, phenomena in terms of the meanings people bring to them.
Qualitative research involves the studied use and collection of a variety of
empirical materials . . . that describe routine and problematic moments
and meanings in individuals' lives. Accordingly, qualitative researchers
deploy a wide range of interconnected methods, hoping always to get a
better fix on the subject matter at hand.

(Denzin and Lincoln 1994: 2)

The authors contributing to the series are established, well-known
researchers with a wealth of experience on which to draw and all make use
of specific and vivid examples from their own and others' work. A consequence of this use of examples is the way in which each writer conveys a
sense of research being an intensely satisfying and enjoyable activity, in spite
of the specific difficulties that are sometimes encountered.

Whilst they differ in terms of structure and layout each book deals with:

• The historical background of the approach: how it developed; examples
  of its use; implications for its use at the present time.

- Epistemological issues: the nature of the data produced; the roles of the researcher and the researched.
- Appropriate uses: in what research contexts and for which research questions is the approach most appropriate; where might the research be inappropriate or unlikely to yield the best data.

They then describe and discuss using the approach in educational settings, looking at such matters as:

- How to do it: designing and setting up the research; planning and preparation; negotiating access; likely problems; technical details; recording of data.
- Ethical considerations: the roles of and the relationship between the researcher and the researched; ownership of data; issues of honesty.
- Data analysis.
- Presentation of findings: issues to do with writing up and presenting findings.

In suggesting that biographical approaches in general, and life history methods in particular are eminently suitable for studying many topics relating to schools, schooling and education, Ivor Goodson and Pat Sikes are clearly at odds with the line taken by the Secretary of State for Education when he said,

> We're not interested in worthless correlations based on small samples from which it is impossible to draw generalizable conclusions. We welcome large scale, quantitative information on effect sizes which will allow us to generalize, with in-depth case studies into how processes work
>
> (Blunkett 2000)

Life history studies can and often do, have a 'sample' of one and they rarely, if ever, involve the sorts of numbers that give any meaning to statistical analyses. And yet, as *Life History Research in Educational Settings: Learning from Lives* shows, such research does seem to be especially useful to those attempting to make sense of topics and issues related to education, and particularly, of how individuals and groups perceive and experience aspects of this intensely personal and relationship based area of social life.

Life history has had a chequered history. Initially lauded as productive of 'the *perfect* type of sociological material' (Thomas and Znaniecki 1918–1920: 1832), the approach fell out of favour, primarily as a result of the ascendancy of positivist approaches but also because it is time consuming and labour intensive: it is a costly method. In the 1970s however, interest in and use of, auto/biographical and narrative methods and methodology began to increase (in all parts of the world, it would seem) and now, as we enter the new millennium, studies using them are by no means unusual. Nowhere has this renaissance been more apparent than in educational studies and, inter alia, life history has been used to explore the experiences, motivations and values of different groups of teachers, initial professional socialization and continuing professional development, school management and organization, curriculum development, pedagogical practices and policy implementation. There has also been considerable discussion of associated epistemological and methodological issues and problems. These studies and discussions have tended to be reported in journal articles and in edited collections, although there are a number of monographs dealing with specific projects. *Life History Research in Educational Settings: Learning from Lives* is somewhat different in that it combines accounts of research with information about how to do life history whilst also considering methodological and epistemological issues and concerns.

Final note

It was Barry Troyna who initially came up with the idea for this series. Although his publishing career was extensive, Barry had never been a series editor and, in his inimitable way, was very keen to become one. Whilst he was probably best known for his work in the field of 'race', Barry was getting increasingly interested in issues to do with methodology when he became ill with the cancer which was eventually to kill him. It was during the twelve months of his illness that he and I drew up a proposal and approached potential authors. All of us knew that it was very likely that he would not live to see the series in print but he was adamant that it should go ahead, nonetheless. The series is, therefore, something of a memorial to him and royalties from it will be going to the Radiotherapy Unit at the Walsgrave Hospital in Coventry.

Pat Sikes

References

Blunkett, D. (2001) Influence or Irrelevance: can social science improve government? Speech to the ESRC, February 2.

Denzin, N. and Lincoln, Y. (1994) Introduction: entering the field of qualitative research, in N. Denzin and Y. Lincoln (eds) *Handbook of Qualitative Research*, California: Sage.

Hargreaves, D. (1996) *Teaching as a Research-Based Profession: Possibilities and Prospects*, TTA Annual lecture. London: TTA.

Slee, R., Weiner, G. with Tomlinson, S. (eds) (1998) Introduction: school effectiveness for whom?, in *School Effectiveness for Whom? Challenges to the School Effectiveness and School Improvement Movements*, pp. 1–9. London: Falmer.

Thomas, W. and Znaniecki, F. (1918–1920) *The Polish Peasant in Europe and America*, 2nd edn. Chicago: University of Chicago Press.

Troyna, B. (1994) Blind Faith? Empowerment and Educational Research, *International Studies in the Sociology of Education*, 4(1): 3–24.

Acknowledgements

As always, we could not have written this book without the help of a host of people. Nicky Skivington is top of the list for her work in the preparation and laborious task of editing and checking the manuscript. Given Pat's ineptitude with email attachments and Ivor's peripatetic professional lifestyle, this was no mean feat. Shona Mullen, at Open University Press, has been caring and patient over and beyond the call of duty, as has her colleague Anita West. (It is interesting that the conception and birth of this book took far longer than it took Shona and Tony to produce Melissa!)

Our personal thank-yous are as follows:

For Ivor:
To all the colleagues in the University of East Anglia, a supportive 'conversational community'; in particular to Nigel Norris for his unstinting academic and administrative support over many years, and to Rob Walker who first awakened my interest in life histories. Last, but definitely not least, to my much loved twosome, Mary and son Andy (as he builds his life history, he has one very proud dad).

And for Pat:
To 'old' colleagues at the Institute of Education, University of Warwick, especially Wendy Robinson, and new ones at the School of Education, University of Sheffield; to students and ex-students who have 'road-tested' extracts; to Robyn and Joby who like to see their names in books; and to HT, Alan and OLW for continuing inspiration, love, support and care.

Introduction

Over the years since 1983, when we first met at a conference on the theme of teachers' lives and careers, we have had numerous conversations about why we are so attracted to life history research. Although we are perfectly able to construct academic justifications for using the approach, we know full well that the major motivating force is that we are both incurably and insatiably curious about other people's lives. Nothing interests either of us more than listening to life stories, considering them in the various settings in which they occurred, then teasing out and exploring possible influences and explanations, interpretations and alternatives, silences and significances. This, in our view, is the essence of the approach: life historians examine how individuals talk about and story their experiences and perceptions of the social contexts they inhabit.

Basically, life historians are concerned with inviting their informants to consider and articulate answers to questions like: Who are you? What are you? Why are you? Why do you think, believe, do, make sense of the world and the things that happen to you, as you do? Why have these particular things happened to you? Why has your life taken the course that it has? Where is it likely to go? What is your total experience like in relation to the experiences of other people? What are the differences and similarities? Why are there differences and similarities? How does your life articulate with those of others within the various social worlds you inhabit? What are the influences on your life and what influence and impact do you have? What is the meaning of life? How do you story your life? Why do you story it in this way? What resources do you employ in assembling your life story?

It is easy to get carried away and to slip into comic parody when asking what might be described as the 'big' questions about people's experiences and understandings of the world, their place, or rather places, within it and the things which happen to them. Sometimes, perhaps, the joking serves a defensive function: it is almost a survival strategy to enable us to cope with the enormity and, hence, the scariness of what it is that we are asking, because there is no doubt that these are questions to which there are unlikely to be easy or straightforward answers. These are questions which deal with the essence of identity, of our place in the world – with the purpose and meaning of it all – and it is possible that some answers may be, at best, unflattering to our sense of self and, at worst, lead to despair, alienation and anomie. On the other hand, there may be no answers in a definitive sense. In any case, our answers are dependent upon our faith and belief in the veracity and power of whatever fundamental theories of social life and explanations of human action/behaviour we may subscribe to: in other words, upon our ontological and epistemological positions and assumptions.

If you were to ask those who make use of life history approaches what their fundamental beliefs and understandings were, the chances are that you would get many, many different answers. However, one thing that all would agree on would be that, as Michael Erben (1998a: 1) puts it: 'individual motivations and social influences have no easy demarcation'. Life historians believe that the stories people tell about their lives can give important insights and provide vital entry points into the 'big' questions aforementioned, and the implications that responses to these questions have for enquiry into any aspect of social life (*ibid.* 1998b). They use the life history method for the following reasons:

1 It explicitly recognizes that lives are not hermetically compartmentalized into, for example, the person we are at work (the professional self) and who we are at home (parent/child/partner selves), and that, consequently, anything which happens to us in one area of our lives potentially impacts upon and has implications for other areas too.
2 It acknowledges that there is a crucial interactive relationship between individuals' lives, their perceptions and experiences, and historical and social contexts and events.
3 It provides evidence to show how individuals negotiate their identities and, consequently, experience, create and make sense of the rules and roles of the social worlds in which they live.

Social life is extremely complex, and attempts to explain it through analytical categories or formulae (of the $a + b = c$ variety) should always be offered simply as frameworks for comprehension with explicit recognition of their limitations. Like Patricia Clough, we take the view that: 'all factual representations of reality, even statistical representations are narratively constructed' (Clough 1992: 2). In other words, any attempts to interpret and re-present the world can be seen as one way, using a particular language rather than another, of telling the story. It seems to us that 'scientific' or 'technical vocabulary' is usually inadequate and inappropriate when it comes to expressing human emotions which are, after all, at the heart of human perception and experience. Life historians work from what people say, using the language they use to express and describe their lives. Of course, the relationship between what they say and 'reality', 'actuality', 'truth' is not straightforward, and it is certainly not our intention to suggest that we believe that life historians have found the methodological equivalent of the Holy Grail, the key to unlock 'true' and complete answers about the human condition. We do believe, however, that it does have a major contribution to make to many investigations of aspects of life in social and educational settings, not least, because of the way in which life history accounts can, and should, be readable and accessible, enabling researchers, informants and readers to gain a recognizable impression of how particular lives are lived and expressed in a day-to-day context.

Our aim for this book, therefore, is to describe and discuss life history method and related issues which seem to be particularly pertinent, and to provide pointers as to how to use it and the ways in which it might be used in educational settings. We do not necessarily expect people to read this book through from start to finish. Whilst chapters do refer to each other, our intention has been to deal with each topic in a relatively self-contained way, recognizing that readers come to a text with different needs. The following outline of contents is, therefore, meant as a guide.

The first chapter, 'Developing life histories', tells the story of the rise and fall and rehabilitation of life history method and makes a case for why it is particularly suited to educational studies of all kinds, whatever their specific or substantive focus. The chapter addresses the relevance of life histories to the 'condition of postmodernity'.

Chapter 2, 'Techniques for doing life history', deals with operational, practical and technical details. The aim is to show readers what life history research and data can be like. We have chosen to place this section early in the book in order to provide a substantive basis that informs and illustrates subsequent discussions of more theoretical issues. Areas considered include: negotiating access and collaboration; strategies for collecting data (for example, using time-lines, group work of various kinds, diaries, journals); interviewing practice; recording data; respondent validation; working with data; transcribing; analysis and approaches to data presentation.

Chapter 3, 'What have you got when you've got a life story? Epistemological considerations', looks at issues such as: the nature of life history data (for example: What have you got when you've got a life story? What do you do when you turn it into a history? What is the relationship between a life story as told and the life as lived?); whether life history is 'proper' research (for example, can its findings be regarded as 'valid' and/or 'reliable' and, in any case, are these appropriate concepts to apply to essentially and unashamedly subjectively focused research?); research reflexivity, (for example, in what ways does the very fact that life history research is being done influence the social situations in which it takes place? How is it perceived and experienced by the people it involves and touches, and how do their perceptions and experiences influence and impact upon all stages of the research?)

The fourth chapter, 'Studying teachers' life histories and professional practice', makes considerable use of life history data in order to illustrate how the approach can not only yield information which can broaden our understanding of teachers' professional work, but also be harnessed as a practical strategy for personal and professional development.

Chapter 5, 'Life stories and social context: storylines and scripts', considers how stories which are divorced from historical context can limit our understanding, particularly when focusing on classrooms and teaching. The chapter also looks at how our lives are scripted and constructed in ways that often resonate with the social order and how it is important to disrupt and deconstruct some of these scripted lives in our life history interviews. The role of the life history interview in 'interrupting subjectivity' is described, as is work that assesses the storylines by which people construct their lives.

Embarking upon life history research demands that researchers consider, carefully, the nature of the approach and the implications of being involved in such work for the lives of informants and researchers alike. In Chapter 6, 'Questions of ethics and power in life history research', we look at what this means in a practical sense. We also discuss the notions of empowerment, emancipation and giving voice, as they have been associated with life history research.

The last chapter, 'Confronting the dilemmas', contains a summary discussion of the book's contents. We will also touch on what we have characterized as alternative lives. Lives can take many routes. Speculating on alternative possibilities can give some interesting insights into the actual path that was taken and what that particular path meant for the individual. This is an exciting and new area with considerable potential for future research.

Finally, and above all, we hope that readers gain some sense of our fascination with life history and that they, themselves, should come to share it. Everyone has stories to tell. No life can truly be considered uneventful or boring: and life history helps to remind us of this, as it also shows how individual lives are affected by when, where, how and by whom (in social positioning terms) they are lived. This might sound too obvious a truism to be worth stating, but it seems that, paradoxically, some other methods and approaches to social research fail to acknowledge the essential humanity and personal significance of the people they purport to understand. Our view is that this is not acceptable. Life history helps to guard against it.

References

Clough, P. (1992) *The End(s) of Ethnography*. London: Sage.

Erben, M. (1998a) Introduction, in M. Erben (ed.) *Biography and Education: A Reader*, pp. 1–3. London: Falmer Press.

Erben, M. (1998b) Biography and research methods, in M. Erben (ed.) *Biography and Education: A Reader*, pp. 4–17. London: Falmer Press.

1 | Developing life histories

The story of life history: origins of the life history method

Searching for the origins of the life history method, we find that the first life histories, in the form of autobiographies of American Indian chiefs, were collected by anthropologists at the beginning of the twentieth century (for example, Barrett 1906; Radin 1920). Since then, the approach has been increasingly adopted by sociologists and other scholars working in the humanities, although its popularity and acceptance as a research strategy has tended to wax and wane. As we write, life history and other biographical and narrative approaches are widely seen as having a great deal to offer, and in this chapter we argue that they should be employed in educational studies. But, in examining their scholarly fate, we have to scrutinize their use to date within sociology, as this has been a major 'battleground' in their evolution.

For sociologists, the main landmark in the development of life history methods came in the 1920s, following the publication of Thomas and Znaniecki's (1918–1920) mammoth study, *The Polish Peasant in Europe and America*. In exploring the experience of Polish peasants migrating to the United States, Thomas and Znaniecki relied mainly on migrants' autobiographical accounts, alongside extant diaries and letters. For these authors, life histories were the data *par excellence* of the social scientist, and they present a strident case for using life histories above all other methods:

In analysing the experiences and attitudes of an individual, we always reach data and elementary facts which are exclusively limited to this individual's personality, but can be treated as mere incidences of more or less general classes of data or facts, and can thus be used for the determination of laws of social becoming. Whether we draw our materials for sociological analysis from detailed life records of concrete individuals or from the observation of mass phenomena, the problems of sociological analysis are the same. But even when we are searching for abstract laws, life records, as complete as possible, constitute the *perfect* type of sociological material, and if social science has to use other materials at all it is only because of the practical difficulty of obtaining at the moment a sufficient number of such records to cover the totality of sociological problems, and of the enormous amount of work demanded for an adequate analysis of all the personal materials necessary to characterise the life of a social group. If we are forced to use mass phenomena as material, or any kind of happenings taken without regard to the life histories of the individuals who participated, it is a defect, not an advantage, of our present sociological method.

(Thomas and Znaniecki 1918–1920: 1831–3)

Thomas and Znaniecki's pioneering work established the life history as a bona fide research device (although, as Miller (2000) points out, its foundations can be seen in the notion of historicism as expressed by Wilhelm Dilthey). The prominent position of the life history was further consolidated by the flourishing tradition of sociological research stimulated at Chicago, particularly by Robert Park.

In the range of studies of city life completed under Park, the life history method was strongly in evidence: *The Gang* (Thrasher 1928), *The Gold Coast and the Slum* (Zorbaugh 1929), *The Hobo* (Anderson 1923) and *The Ghetto* (Wirth 1928). But perhaps the zenith was reached in the 1930s with publications such as Clifford Shaw's account of a 'mugger' in *The Jack-Roller* (Shaw 1930), and Edwin Sutherland's *The Professional Thief* (Cornwell and Sutherland 1937). Howard Becker's comments on Shaw's study underline one of the major strengths of the life history method:

By providing this kind of voice from a culture and situation that are ordinarily not known to intellectuals generally and to sociologists in particular, *The Jack Roller* enables us to improve our theories at the most profound level: by putting ourselves in Stanley's skin, we can feel and become aware of the deep biases about such people that ordinarily permeate our thinking and shape the kinds of problems we investigate. By truly entering into Stanley's life, we can begin to see what we take for granted (and ought not to) in designing our research – what kinds of assumptions about delinquents, slums and Poles are embedded in the way we set the questions we study.

(Becker 1970: 71)

Becker's argument goes to the heart of the appeal of life history methods at their best: for life history data disrupts the normal assumptions of what is 'known' by intellectuals in general, and sociologists in particular. Conducted successfully, the life history forces a confrontation with other people's subjective perceptions. This confrontation can be avoided, and so often is avoided in many other social scientific methods: one only has to think of the common rush to the quantitative indicator or theoretical construct, to the statistical table or the ideal type. This sidesteps the messy confrontation with human subjectivity which we believe should comprise the heartland of the sociological enterprise. Behind and/or coterminous with this methodological sidestep, there is often a profound substantive and political sidestep. In the avoidance of human subjectivity, quantitative assessment and theoretical commentaries can so easily service powerful constituencies within the social and economic order. As we shall see, this tendency to favour and support power is always a potential problem in social science and later we will discuss some of the safeguards that can be employed in life history work.

From the statement about 'putting ourselves in Stanley's skin', Becker leads on to the assertion that Stanley's story offers the possibility 'to begin to ask questions about delinquency from the point of view of the delinquent' (*ibid.*: 71), so that it follows that questions will be asked not from the point of view of the powerful actors but from the perspective of those who are 'acted upon' in professional transactions. These are, then, some important reasons, which move beyond the issues of methodological debate, as to why life history methods might be unpopular in some quarters.

Life history, by its nature, asserts and insists that 'power' should listen to the people it claims to serve, as Becker notes:

> If we take Stanley seriously, as his story must impel us to do, we might well raise a series of questions that have been relatively little studied – questions about the people who deal with delinquents, the tactics they use, their suppositions about the world, and the constraints and pressures they are subject to.
>
> (*ibid.*: 71)

However, this contention should be read in the light of Shaw's own 'early warning' in his preface, where he cautions the reader 'against drawing conclusions' about general causes of delinquency on the basis of a single case record.

One of the best early attempts to analyse the methodological base of the life history method was Dollard's (1949) *Criteria for the Life History*. Foreshadowing Becker, he argued that: 'detailed studies of the lives of individuals will reveal new perspectives on the culture as a whole which are not accessible when one remains on the formal cross sectional plane of observation' (p. 4). A lot of Dollard's arguments have a familiar ring, perhaps reflecting the influence of George Herbert Mead. He notes that:

> as soon as we take the post of observer on the cultural level the individual is lost in the crowd and our concepts never lead us back to him. After we have 'gone cultural' we experience the person as a fragment of

a (derived) culture pattern, as a marionette dancing on the strings of (reified) culture forms.

(Dollard 1949: 5)

In contrast to this, the life historian: 'can see his life history subject as a link in a chain of social transmission' (*ibid*.: 5). This linkage should ensure that life history methods will ameliorate the 'presentism' which exists in so much sociological theory and a good deal of symbolic interactionism (this is explored later in the chapter). Dollard describes this linkage between historical past, present and future:

There were links before him from which he acquired his present culture. Other links will follow him to which he will pass on the current of tradition. The life history attempts to describe a unit in that process: it is a study of one of the strands of a complicated collective life which has historical continuity.

(*ibid*.: 15)

Dollard is especially good, though perhaps unfashionably polemical, in his discussion of the tension between what might be called the 'cultural legacy', the weight of collective tradition and expectation, and the individual's unique history and capacity for interpretation and action. By focusing on this tension, Dollard argues, the life history offers a way of exploring the relationship between the culture, the social structure and individual lives. This is a similar argument to that developed later in Chapter 5 on life stories and social context, where structure and agency are shown to collide around cultural storylines. Thus, Dollard believed that in the best life history work:

we must constantly keep in mind the situation both as defined by others and by the subject, such a history will not only define both versions but let us see clearly the pressure of the formal situation and the force of the inner private definition of the situation.

(*ibid*.: 32)

This resolution, or attempt to address a common tension, is seen as valuable because:

whenever we encounter difference between our official or average or cultural expectation of action in a 'situation' and the actual conduct of the person this indicates the presence of a private interpretation.

(*ibid*.: 32)

In fact, Dollard was writing some time after a decline set in for life history methods (one of the unfortunate side-effects of this is that Dollard's work is not as well known as it should be). After reaching its peak in the 1930s, the life history approach fell from grace and was largely abandoned by social scientists. This was primarily because the increasingly powerful advocacy of statistical methods gained them a growing number of adherents among sociologists; also, ethnographically inclined sociologists began to place more emphasis on situation than on biography as the basis for understanding human behaviour.

Then, in the 1970s, something of a 'minor resurgence' (Plummer 1990) could be observed, starting, particularly and significantly, among deviancy sociologists. Thus, there were studies of a transsexual (Bogdan 1974), a professional fence (Klockars 1975) and, with a fine sense of history following Shaw's 1930 study, once again, a professional thief (Chambliss 1972).

Whilst life history methods have long been popular with journalists-cum-sociologists like Studs Terkel in the United States, Jeremy Seabrook and Ronald Blythe in the UK, and a growing band of 'oral Historians' (Thompson 1978, 1988), Daniel Bertaux's (1981) collection, *Biography and Society,* marked a significant step in the academic rehabilitation of the approach. This book was closely followed by Ken Plummer's (1983) important *Documents of Life* (a revised version of which was published in 2000), and Tierney's (1998) special issue of *Qualitative Inquiry* is also of interest here.

Feminist researchers have been particularly vociferous in their support of the approach, owing mainly to the way in which it can be used to give expression to, and celebration of, hidden or 'silenced' lives (cf. McLaughlin and Tierney 1993): lives which are lived privately and without public accomplishment – the sorts of lives most women (and, it has to be said, most men) live (cf. Personal Narratives Group 1989; Stanley 1990, 1992; Gluck and Patai 1991; Middleton 1997; Munro 1998; Weiler and Middleton 1999). Similarly, those researching issues and aspects of sexuality, notably, Plummer (1995) and Sparkes (1994), have also made considerable use of the approach.

Within the field of educational studies, working with teachers and pupils who are, again, arguably marginal in terms of their social power, life history has been seen as particularly useful and appropriate because, as Bullough (1998: 20–1) points out, 'public and private cannot . . . be separated in teaching . . . The person comes through when teaching'. Life history does not ask for such separation: indeed it demands holism. The growing number of life history studies dealing with educational topics is testimony to this (for example, Ball and Goodson 1985; Sikes *et al.* 1985; Goodson 1992a; Casey 1993; Middleton 1993; Goodson and Hargreaves 1996; Osler 1997; Sikes 1997; Erben 1998b; Kridel 1998).

Among these scholars, albeit in marginal or fragmented groups, a debate is under way which promises a thoroughgoing re-examination of the potential of life history methods. But, before we consider the contemporary appeal of the life history, it is important to discover why life history method was for so long eclipsed by social theory, social survey and by participant observation. In this examination, the emphasis will be on distinguishing fundamental methodological stumbling blocks from professional, micro-political and personal reasons for the decline of life history work. Often the latter are far more important than those involved in the methodological 'paradigm wars' acknowledge.

Reasons for the decline of the life history in early sociological study

By 1966, Becker was able to summarize the fate of the life history method among American sociologists in this manner: 'given the variety of scientific uses to which the life history may be put, one must wonder at the relative neglect into which it has fallen' (Becker 1970: 71–2).

Becker noted that sociologists have never given up life histories altogether, but neither have they made it one of their standard research tools. The general pattern was, and by and large continues to be, that: 'they know of life history studies and assign them for their students to read. But they do not ordinarily think of gathering life history documents or of making the technique part of their research approach' (*ibid.*: 71–2).

The reasons for the decline of life history methods are partly specific to the Chicago department. From the late 1920s, life histories came under increasing fire as the debate within the department between the virtues of case study (and life histories) and statistical techniques intensified. Faris (1967), in his study of Chicago sociology, records a landmark within this debate:

> To test this issue, Stouffer had hundreds of students write autobiographies instructing them to include everything in their life experiences relating to school usage and the prohibition law. Each of these autobiographies was read by a panel of persons presumed to be qualified in life history research, and for each subject the reader indicated on a scaled line the position of the subject's attitude regarding prohibition. Inter-reader agreement was found to be satisfactory. Each of the same subjects had also filled out a questionnaire that formed a scale of the Thurstone type. The close agreement of the scale measurement of each subject's attitude with the reader's estimate of the life history indicated that, as far as the scale score was concerned, nothing was gained by the far more lengthy and laborious process of writing and judging a life history.
>
> (Faris 1967: 114–15)

One might note that the experiment does beg the question of why use life history simply in order to measure attitude. No doubt the autobiographies *did* contain explanations of 'why' the informants' attitudes were of a particular degree: such information could be valuable for purposes other than attitude measurement and would, moreover, not be accessible by means of a questionnaire.

Even within Chicago case study work, the life history declined against other ethnographic devices, notably participant observation. One element of the explanation of this lies, perhaps, in the orientations of Blumer and Hughes. These two sociologists provide a bridge between the Chicago school of the 1920s and 1930s and those Matza has termed the 'neo-Chicagoans', such as Becker (1970). Blumer's symbolic interactionism places primary emphasis on process and situation, and explanations in terms of biography, like those in terms of social structural forces, are regarded with considerable suspicion. Hughes's comparative approach to the study of occupations may have tended to limit interest in biography in favour of a concern with the typical problems faced by occupational practitioners and the strategies they adopt for dealing with them. An additional factor, which hastened the decline of the methodological eclecticism of Chicago sociology with the life history playing a central role, was the decline of Chicago itself as a dominant centre for sociological studies.

The fate of life history methods has been inextricably linked to the historical emergence of sociology as a discipline. Hence, the methodological weaknesses of the approach came to be set against the need to develop abstract theory. When sociology was highly concerned with providing detailed accounts of specific communities, institutions or organizations, such weaknesses were clearly of less account. But in the life history of sociology, the pervasive drift of academic disciplines towards abstract theory has been irresistibly followed: in this evolutionary imperative it is not difficult to discern the desire of sociologists to gain parity of esteem with other academic disciplines. The resulting pattern of mainstream sociology meant that sociologists came to pursue 'data formulated in the abstract categories of their own theories rather than in the categories that seemed most relevant to the people they studied' (Becker 1970: 72).

Alongside the move towards abstract academic theory, sociological method became more 'professional'. Essentially, this led towards a model of 'single-study' research, defined by Becker in this way:

> I use the term to refer to research projects that are conceived of as self-sufficient and self-contained, which provide all the evidence one needs to accept or reject the conclusions they proffer . . . The single study is integrated with the main body of knowledge in the following way: it derives its hypotheses from an inspection of what is already known: then, after the research is completed, if those hypotheses have been demonstrated, they are added to the wall of what is already scientifically known and used as the basis for further studies. The important point is that the researcher's hypothesis is either proved or disproved on the basis of what he has discovered in doing that one piece of research.
> (Becker 1970: 72)

The imperative towards this pattern of sociological research can be clearly evidenced in the traditions and organizational format of emergent professional sociology. The PhD student must define and test their hypothesis; the journal article must test the author's own or other academics' hypotheses; the research project or programme must state the generalizable aims and locate the burden of what has to be proved. But this dominant experimental model, so fruitful in analogies with other *sciences* and, hence, so crucial in legitimating sociology as a fully-fledged academic discipline, led to the neglect of sociology's full range of methodology and data sources.

> It has led people to ignore the other functions of research and particularly to ignore the contribution made by one study to an overall research enterprise even when the study, considered in isolation, produced no definitive results of its own. Since, by these criteria, the life history did not produce definitive results, people have been at a loss to make anything of it and by and large have declined to invest the time and effort necessary to acquire life history documents.
>
> (*ibid.*: 73)

Becker ends by holding out the hope that sociologists will, in the future, develop a 'further understanding of the complexity of the scientific enterprise' (p. 73); that this will rehabilitate the life history method and lead to a new range of life history documents as generative as those produced by the Chicago sociologists in the 1920s and 1930s.

In the period following Becker's strictures in 1970, sociology was subject to a number of new directions which sought to re-embrace some of the elements lost in the 'positivist', theory-testing models. (Morris 1977; Cuff and Payne 1979). One new direction which clearly stressed biography, the phenomenological sociology of Berger and Luckmann (Berger 1963; Berger and Luckmann 1967), actually resulted in little empirical work.

Hence, research in interpretive sociology has displayed a heavy emphasis on situation under the influence of interactionism and ethnomethodology. The paradox is that these new directions in sociology moved away from the 'positivist' model, but directly to situation and occasion; as a result, life history and biography have tended to remain at the sidelines of the sociological enterprise. For instance, interactionist studies have focused on the perspectives and definitions emerging among groups of actors in particular situations, the backcloth to this being presented as a somewhat monolithic 'structural' or 'cultural legacy' which constrains, in a rather disconnected manner, the actors' potentialities. In overreacting to more deterministic models, this situational emphasis most commonly fails to make any connection with historical process. Thus, whilst interactionists retained their interest in the meaning that objects had for actors, these meanings increasingly came to be seen as collectively generated to deal with specific situations, rather than as the product of individual or even collective biography.

Viewing sociology's evolution over half a century or so provides a number of insights into the life history method. Firstly, as sociologists began to take seriously their social scientific pursuit of generalizable facts and the development of abstract theory, life history work came to be seen as having serious methodological flaws. In addition, since life history studies often appeared to be only 'telling tales', these methodological reservations were enhanced by the generally low status of this as an 'academic' or 'scientific' exercise. Paradoxically, even when antidotes to the experimental model of sociology developed, these took the form of interactionism and ethno-methodology, both of which stressed situation and occasion rather than biography and background. Moreover, since these new directions had status problems of their own, life history work was unattractive on this count as well. At the conference, where Ivor Goodson's early work on life history was originally delivered as a seminar paper, a classroom interactionist rejected the exhortation to consider life history work by saying: 'we should not suggest new methodologies of this sort . . . because of the problem of our academic careers. Christ! Ethnography is low status enough as it is' (Goodson 1983).

Set against the life history of the aspirant academic, keen to make a career in the academy as it is, or as it has been shaped and ordered, we clearly see the unattractiveness of the life history method at particular stages in the evolution of sociology. But, by the 1980s, matters were beginning to change markedly in ways that have led to a re-embracing of life history methods.

From modernism to postmodernism

Under modernism, life history languished because it persistently failed the 'objectivity tests': numbers were not collected and statistical aggregation produced and, since studies were not judged to be representative or exemplary, contributions to theory remained parsimonious. In the historical aspiration to be a social 'science', life history failed its membership test.

However, as Harvey (1989) and others have documented, the 'condition of postmodernity' provides both new dilemmas and new directions. In some ways, the new possibilities invert the previous deficits which were perceived in life history work. In moving from objectivities to subjectivities, new prospects open for life history work and, as a result, a range of new studies has begun to appear (see Denzin and Lincoln 1994a, 2000). As is often the case, educational studies have been slow to follow new directions, although new work has recently begun to emerge.

Life history work has accompanied the turn to postmodernism and post-structuralism, particularly as evidenced in sociological studies, gender studies, cultural studies, literacy theory and even psychology. Such work facilitates the move away from modernist master narratives which are viewed as social productions of the Enlightenment Project. Alongside this move, the notion of a singular, knowable, essential self is judged as part of the social production of individualism and one linked to agentic selves in pursuit of progress, knowingness and emancipation. Assumptions of linearity of chronological timelines and storylines are challenged in favour of more multiple, disrupted notions of subjectivity. Foucault's work, for instance, has focused sociological attention on the way in which institutions like hospitals and prisons regulate and constitute our subjectivities. Likewise, discourse studies have focused on the role of language in constructing identities in producing textual representations which purport to 'capture' the essential selves of others (Shotter and Gergen 1989).

These new syntagms in sociological work have led to a revival in the use of life history work:

> The current focus on acknowledging the subjective, multiple and partial nature of human experience has resulted in a revival of life history methodology. What were previously criticisms of life history, its lack of representativeness and its subjective nature, are now its greatest strength.
>
> (Munro 1998: 8)

Yet, the postmodern concern with disrupting constructed selves and stories is itself not without difficulty, as Munro reflectively notes:

> In collecting the life histories of women teachers I find myself situated in a paradoxical position. I know that I cannot 'collect' a life. Narrative does not provide a better way to locate truth, but in fact reminds us that all good stories are predicated on the quality of the fiction. We live many lives. Consequently, the life histories in this book do not present neat, chronological accounts of women's lives. This would be an act of betrayal, a distortion, a continued form of 'fitting' women's lives into the fictions, categories and cultural norms of patriarchy. Instead, my understanding of a life history suggests that we need to attend to the silences as well as what is said, that we need to attend to how the story is told as well as what is told or not told, and to attend to the tensions and contradictions rather than succumb to the temptations to gloss over these in our desire for 'the' story.
>
> (ibid.: 12–13)

Here, Munro begins to address the methodological and, indeed, ethical minefield which potentially confronts, confuses and confounds the researcher and the researched. Michelle Fine has written of some of the issues to be confronted:

> Self and Other are knottily entangled. This relationship, as lived between researchers and informants, is typically obscured in social science texts, protecting privilege, securing distance, and laminating the

contradictions . . . Slipping into a contradictory discourse of individualism, persona-logic theorizing, and de-contextualization, we inscribe the
Other, strain to white out Self, and refuse to engage the contradictions
that litter our texts.

(Fine 1994: 72)

Fine's warnings are of inestimable value as we approach life history work.
But in the end we do face the inevitable closure of the text that is produced,
or are for ever caught in the politics of infinite regress where every closure
must be reopened. For Fine warns us that the search for the complete and
coherent is a delusion; we produce a snapshot of transgressions in process
when we write up life history work.

Furthermore, the relationship of the researcher and informant is much
concerned in the postmodern predilection for 'rejection of the unitary subject for a more complex, multiple and contradictory notion of subjectivity'
(Munro 1998: 35). What does such researcher rejection mean in the face
of an informant who narrates their life as a search for coherence? For it
remains the case that many people narrate their lives according to an aspiration for coherence, for a unitary self. Should we, in Munro's words 'reject'
this social construction of self? Rejection is not the issue here, for life history
work should, where possible, refuse to play postmodern God. Life history
work is interested in the way people *do* narrate their lives, not in the way
they *should*. Here it seeks to avoid the fate of some postmodern funda-
mentalists.

Life stories, then, are the starting point for our work. Such stories are, in
their nature, already removed from life experiences: they are lives interpreted and made textual. They represent a partial, selective commentary on
lived experience. Freeman has explored some of the issues that are raised
here:

> For what we will have before us are not lives themselves, but rather
> *texts* of lives, literary artifacts that generally seek to recount in some
> fashion what these lives were like. In this respect, we will be – we must
> be – at least one step removed from the lives that we will be exploring:
> we can only proceed with our interpretive efforts on the basis of what
> has been written [or related] by those whose lives they are.
>
> The basic situation, I hasten to emphasize, obtains not only in the
> case of literary texts of the sort we will be examining here, but in the
> case of interviews and the like along with the observation of human
> action more generally. Interviews, of the sort that social scientists often
> gather, are themselves texts, and while they may not have quite as much
> literary flourish as those we buy in bookstores, they are in their own
> right literary artifacts, taking the form of words, designed to give shape
> to some feature of experience. As for the observation of human action,
> the story is actually much the same: human action, which occurs in time

and yields consequences the significance of which frequently extend beyond the immediate situation in which it takes place, is itself a kind of text; it is a constellation of meanings which, not unlike literary texts or interviews, calls forth the process of interpretation (see especially Ricoeur 1980). In any case, the long and short of this brief excursion into 'textuality' is that our primary interpretive takeoff point will not be lives as such but the words used to speak them.

(Freeman 1998: 7)

The rendering of lived experience into a 'life story' is one interpretive layer, but the move to 'life history' adds a second layer and a further interpretation. Goodson (1992a) has written before of the distinction between stage one, where the informant relates their 'life story' and stage two, where a 'life history' is constructed employing a new range of interviews and documentary data. The move from life story to life history involves the range of methodologies and ethical issues noted earlier. Moving from personal life stories to life histories involves issues of process and power as Bertaux has noted (1981: 9): 'What is really at stake is the relationship between the sociologist and the people who make his work possible by accepting to be interviewed on their life experiences'.

Moving from life story to life history involves a move to account for historical context – a dangerous move, for it offers the researcher considerable 'colonizing' power to 'locate' the life story with all its inevitable selections, shifts and silences. Nonetheless, we hold to the need for providing historical contexts for reading 'life stories'.

Dannefer (1992) has written of the various meanings of context in studying developmental discourse. Here, our concern is to provide communications that cover the social histories and, indeed, social geographies in which life stories are embedded: without contextual commentary on issues of time and space, life stories remain uncoupled from the conditions of their social construction. This, above all, is the argument for life histories rather than life stories.

Whilst rightly concerned about the colonizing dangers of contextual commentary, even poststructuralist accounts often end up moving from life stories to life histories, and they confront issues surrounding the changing contexts of time and space. For instance, Middleton's early work on women teachers' lives relates a substantive account of one feminist teacher's pedagogy within the specific sociocultural setting of post-Second World War New Zealand (Middleton 1992). Likewise Munro, an avowed feminist poststructuralist, argues that:

Since this study is concerned with placing the lives of women teachers within a broader historical context, historical data regarding the communities and the time period in which they taught was also collected. Although I am not an educational historian an attempt was made to understand both the local history and broader historical context in which these women lived.

(Munro 1998: 11)

The distinction between life stories or narratives and life histories is, then, a crucial one. By providing contextual data, the life stories can be seen in the light of changing patterns of time and space in testimony and action as social constructions.

In this chapter, our aim has been to provide a general overview of the development and use of life history method. In a number of places, we have anticipated issues and themes which will be revisited in subsequent chapters. We now move on to consider pragmatical issues by looking at techniques for doing life history.

2 | Techniques for doing life history

Introduction

The sections dealing with practical procedures and considerations have been placed towards the beginning of the book because we believe that an awareness of what life history research and data can be like will help to inform and illustrate subsequent discussions focusing on more theoretical matters. Having said this, we do want to emphasize a point to which we will regularly return: namely, that we see any separation of theoretical, methodological, practical, epistemological, ethical, ontological (and so on) aspects of research to be in essence artificial. All are, or should be, a considered part of any researcher's whole philosophy of, and approach to, their work. This is true regardless of the paradigm they adopt or methods they use. Addressing each aspect individually, however, does help to provide an organizational framework for comprehension and enables readers to refer more easily and quickly to specific issues or areas. Similarly, whilst at times we may adopt a sequential approach in describing the various stages and phases involved when doing life history research, we know that research does not often happen in a neat, linear manner, and nor is this necessarily desirable.

We are also keen to make it clear that we do not believe that there is only one, 'proper' way of doing life history research. Different projects will have their own features and requirements and each researcher is likely to have their own personal style and a unique emotional engagement with any particular project (see Coffey 1999). Indeed, the extent to which life history methodology is individualistic and personal, relying as it does on 'intensely idiosyncratic personal dynamics' (Sikes *et al.* 1996: 43) is a defining characteristic of the approach. This does mean, though, that it is a methodology that cannot easily be taught 'because . . . personal dynamics are themselves unpackagable' (*ibid.*: 44). An important implication of this is that not everyone can or should do life history research or, as is discussed in a later chapter, can or should use life history to investigate particular topics at particular points in their own life. In any case, if they do use it when they 'cannot' or 'should not', then they are unlikely to succeed for the following reasons:

1 They are unlikely to develop the sort of relationship with informants that tends to lead to 'quality' data.
2 They are unlikely to be sufficiently sensitive to the central tenet of the approach – that, potentially at least, all aspects of life interact with and have implications for each other – to be able to make insightful use of the data.
3 They may even have a negative effect (to a greater or lesser degree, and in a variety of possible life areas) on their informants.

It may seem somewhat contradictory to be writing this book having raised these points because we seem to be saying: 'if you have not got the right sort of personal characteristics then you cannot do this type of research'. Whilst we stand by our claim that not everyone can do life history work, we believe that people can develop and improve their practice by learning from the experiences of others as presented here. Furthermore, one of our key aims is to alert readers to these sensitive issues and, thereby, provide them with a basis for deciding whether or not it is an approach they consider to be appropriate to their particular interests, personality and life stage.

As a general rule, life history research is more likely to appeal to the incurably curious who are interested in, and fascinated by, the minutiae of others' lives, and particularly in how people make sense of their experiences and of the world around them. At the risk of stereotyping (yet on the basis of an informal survey), life historians are likely to prefer novels such as: *A Suitable Boy*, *The Magic Mountain* and *A la Recherche du temps perdu*, to exciting, action-packed yarns. Life history is an approach best suited to people who are able to listen attentively and beyond what is actually being said, and who can ask pertinent questions in a non-threatening manner. It demands the willingness to share one's own experiences, if this seems appropriate, and, of supreme importance, it requires the researcher to be the sort of person that people want to talk to.

Reasons for choosing research approaches and methods

Personal preferences and predilections aside, the key reason for using any research method has to be that it is the most appropriate one, the one most likely to produce data which address, answer or otherwise meet and fulfil the questions, aims and purposes of a specific enquiry. Methods also have to be feasible in terms of time, cost, resources, and within the various parameters of particular research contexts. Tempting though it may be to indulge oneself, as Robson (1993: 26) notes: one of the things that 'unsuccessful research starts with . . . [is] **Method or technique**. Using it as a vehicle to carry out a specific method of investigation'. Research which is 'method-led' can be uneconomical, inappropriate and unjustifiably biased.

However, aficionados of life history would argue that the method can be used effectively to provide useful data on practically every social issue and aspect of life: as we have already noted in Chapter 1, Thomas and Znaniecki (1918–1920) suggested that personal life records do appear to constitute the perfect form of sociological data. To take a slightly ridiculous example, the approach could be used to find out why people buy a specific brand and type of frozen peas. For instance, life history interviews can reveal that some people just pick the nearest package out of the freezer because they have little time to shop, are in a hurry and, because they have a demanding and well-paid job, do not have to worry about cost; others may choose a brand because their mother always bought them and impressed upon her children that these were the best peas to have. Thus, buying Bird's Eye™ petit pois may be tied up with conceptions of what good mothers do based on positive childhood experiences. Pragmatically, brand choice may be to do with where people live and their access to certain shops carrying particular ranges. In 'poorer' areas, for example, choice tends to be more restricted. Buying a supermarket's own brand, as opposed to Bird's Eye, may be to do with economic circumstances and, thereby, occupational status. Alternatively, as a result of advertising campaigns, shoppers might see a certain brand as fitting in with their lifestyle, or their lifestyle aspirations. And, similarly associated with advertising, their children may put pressure on them to buy fashionable brands, perhaps because they want to present a particular image to friends who come to tea. We may say this is a ridiculous example, but frozen food manufacturers no doubt do conduct biographical type research, often using focus groups in an attempt to achieve maximum sales.

Which research method to use depends on what you want to know. If you are a shopkeeper, then your only concern may be to know what will sell best and, therefore, what you should stock. A straightforward and simple survey to find out the most popular brand would, therefore, meet your needs effectively and economically.

When the focus of enquiry is something more far-reaching and significant than a consumer-preference issue, when it is something like why someone becomes a teacher, or how they cope with imposed change, or why they adopt a particular pedagogical style, or how being a teacher fits in with other aspects of a person's life such as parenthood, or what it means to be a gay or lesbian teacher, or a teacher from an ethnic minority group, the potential of life history is enormous. There are likely to be many influences, experiences and relationships within any teacher's life which have led to their developing a particular philosophy of education and taking on a specific professional identity which informs their work. Then there are the various contexts and conditions within which teachers have to work which further have an effect upon what they do and how they do it. As Robert Bullough (1998: 24) has written: 'to understand educational events, one must confront biography'. If the researcher wants to know 'why', 'how', 'what's it like' and 'what does it mean to you', then they may be well advised to include life history methods among their modes of enquiry. If they want to know 'who', 'where', 'how many' and 'what kind', then it would probably be unnecessary and uneconomical in terms of time and resources to embark on detailed interviewing, resulting in vast quantities of data which have then to be transcribed and analysed.

Of course, life history does not have to be an either/or approach. If circumstances allow, and if it is appropriate, then life history can be combined with other methods to provide yet another perspective on a topic. For instance, a study of how a particular subject – let us take religious education – is taught may use surveys, observation, analysis of textbooks and initial and in-service teacher education syllabi to see trends, patterns and frequencies in curriculum content and pedagogical style; it may also use life history interviews to explore whether and how a teacher's own experiences of religion generally, and religious education specifically, might impact upon how they perceive, experience and relate to their work.

As with all types of research, having decided on a focus and on the appropriate approach, there are a number of practical issues which have to be considered and dealt with. It is these to which we now turn.

Research populations

Sample size

Research samples for life history research are usually quite small. Interviewing, transcription and analysis are time consuming and expensive activities. When there is only one researcher, working on a personal, unfunded project, the resources to interview large numbers of people are rarely available – and this is often the case, because one of the difficulties with life history is persuading funders of its appropriateness. As well as the quantitative predilections that are common, this problem is related to some of the historical battles fought over the legitimacy of life history, especially in Chicago in the 1940s (see Chapter 1). Regardless of economic considerations though, life historians usually, although not inevitably, use life history because they take a particular epistemological position which values the subjective, emic and idiographic (see Goodson 1992b: 9). Thus, they may well argue that large samples are unnecessary and even inappropriate because objective, etic and nomothetic generalization is not the ultimate aim.

The fact that life history samples tend to be small, allied with the sort of philosophical and, therefore, epistemological stance that life historians often take, means that they will rarely talk in terms of samples or research populations, and almost never of subjects. 'Respondent', 'informant', 'participant', or just pseudonyms, are likely to be preferred because they do not have the same 'othering' and homogenizing implications that the traditional research designations do. When, as is usually the case, the research is collaborative, or at least has an interactive dimension, then co-researcher, collaborator, or research partner may be the terms used.

It is impossible to say how many informants should be involved in any project. So much depends on the aims of the research, on the topic, and on what is actually possible. Many life histories, including most of the 'original', 'foundational' or 'germinal' ones, undertaken by members of the Chicago school in the 1920s and 1930s, were of one person and aimed to give detailed insight into a specific individual's perception and experience of their life. A study of one individual is rare in education, partly because of the essentially social and collective nature of the enterprise, although the work of Elbaz (1983), Wolcott (1983) Bullough (1989), Sparkes (1994) and Bullough and Baughman (1997), are among the notable exceptions which demonstrate the value of such research.

If the aim is to reveal shared patterns of experience or interpretation within a group of people who have some characteristic, attribute or experience in common, then ideally sample size will be adequate when:

> sufficient data have been collected and saturation occurs and variation is both accounted for and understood ... In qualitative research, the investigator samples until repetition from multiple sources is obtained.
>
> (Morse 1994: 230)

Thus, adequacy is dependent not upon quantity but upon the richness of the data and the nature of the aspect of life being investigated. Researchers should, however, try to ensure that they include some negative or discrepant examples. Pat's (Sikes 1997) research, which focused on teachers' perceptions of the ways in which parenthood had influenced all aspects of their professional lives, involved 25 informants. This was quite a large group because she wanted to include male and female teachers of various ages from as many sectors of the educational system as possible. However, without exception, every single one of them talked about how their feelings for their students changed once they had their own child so, with regard to this theme, saturation could have been considered to have been attained after five or six interviews.

Bertaux (1981) has written about the discovery of the saturation process. In his work on bakers, he describes how they became aware of the point at which saturation had been achieved:

> while we were conducting our fieldwork, however, we came to realize that a process was taking shape, which seemed to indicate that we had

moved in another realm than the one of traditional sample representativity. This new process could be summarized by saying that every new life story was confirming what the preceding ones had shown. Again and again we were collecting the same story about poor, usually rural backgrounds, about very hard exploitation and training during apprenticeship; about moving from village to town, from town to city, from city to Paris (of course this last feature was to be expected). Again and again we heard about some specific health problems – which many workers, especially the young ones, related to their own physical constitution instead of to their working conditions. And despite our efforts, we still could not find a single adult bakery worker born in Paris or even in its suburbs. What was taking place was a process of *saturation*: on it rests the validity of our sociological assumptions. One life story is only one life story. Thirty life stories of thirty men or women scattered in the whole social structure are only thirty life stories. But thirty life stories of thirty men who have lived their lives in one and the same sector of production (here bakery workers) represent more than thirty isolated life stories; taken together, they tell a different story, at a different level: the history of this sector of production, at the level of its pattern of sociostructural relationships. A single life story stands alone, and it would be hazardous to generalize on the ground of that one alone, as a second life story could immediately contradict those premature generalizations. But several life stories *taken from the same set of sociostructural relations* support each other and make up, all together, a strong body of evidence.

(Bertaux 1981: 187, original emphasis)

Sample selection

Life history research rarely involves a random sample of informants. For a start, the sole aim is seldom to make generalizations and so, therefore, such a group is not required. More particularly, however, it is essential that informants are prepared and able, in terms of both time and articulacy, to talk for extended periods. In addition, the research topic is likely to be focused on a specific social situation, thus requiring informants to have the appropriate knowledge and experience (Erben 1998b: 5). Consequently, sampling is frequently one or more of the following types:

1 *Purposive.* The research is concerned with specific characteristics, attributes or experiences and informants are 'selected' because they meet the criteria.
2 *Opportunistic.* For example, by chance the researcher meets someone who volunteers or who is willing to be an informant.
3 *Convenience.* The researcher has easy access to the informants.

4 *Snowball*. The researcher works with an informant who tells them of friends or colleagues who might be prepared to participate.
5 *Homogeneous*. Everyone who has a common experience, attribute or characteristic. This is likely to occur only when the research focuses on a small group, for example all the black women teachers who belong to a group within a local education authority (Rakhit 1999).
6 *Extreme case*. When the informant's characteristics, attributes or experiences are strikingly different from or in some other way noteworthy compared with others in the potential research population.

As with all types of research, researchers need to think carefully before embarking on a study which involves colleagues, friends, acquaintances or relatives. This is, perhaps, especially pertinent here, given that life history work is likely to involve a non-probability sample. Doing research 'in your own backyard' can have unintended consequences with implications going far beyond the data that are collected. For all sorts of reasons, informants may be cautious about what they reveal, and this can be especially so when they are already in some sort of relationship with the enquirer. When the research solicits information of a personal nature, the potential 'power' that such knowledge gives to the researcher can be considerable: as Madelaine Grumet (1991: 69) notes: 'telling a story to a friend is a risky business; the better the friend, the riskier the business'.

It is possible to take the view that non-probability sampling is biased but, in any case, the concept of bias, and particularly of bias as being negative in a research context, is contested by many qualitative researchers generally, and by life historians in particular (see various authors in Denzin and Lincoln (1994a), for example). We would argue that all human knowledge and experience as expressed through verbal accounts is in essence biased. Everyone sees the world through frames of reference which are developed as a result of their possessing particular attributes, or being situated in particular social, historical, geographical, political, religious (or whatever) contexts which, consequently, lead to various and differing experiences. Researchers have to be reflexive in accounting for their own biases, and reflective and enquiring in identifying possible biases in their informants' stories. Rather than seeking to pretend that any aspect of research can ever be bias free, our recommendation is to acknowledge bias and make every attempt to indicate where it may occur. (For further discussion on these issues, see Shacklock and Smyth 1998; Hammersley 2000.)

Negotiating access and participation

Having identified potential informants, the next stage is to invite them to take part. This may seem a relatively straightforward matter but it does raise a number of questions and issues. Perhaps the most significant of these concerns the research bargain: that is the understanding between the researcher and the informant about what the nature of their relationship is and what each can expect from their mutual participation (see Measor and Sikes 1992: 213; Goodson and Fliesser 1994). Of course, this varies from study to study but, in some cases, participation can involve a considerable commitment on the part of the informant. In the first place, life history interviews can take up many hours. For instance, Bascia (1996: 5) reports a project where informants were interviewed for between 2 and 24 hours. Thus, her work with one male immigrant teacher involved twelve sessions, each of, on average, 2 hours' duration followed by journal and reflection entries that constituted further data. Sikes et al.'s (1985) life history study of art and science, secondary school teachers involved informants in two to seven interviews, each lasting, on average, 1 to 1½ hours. Pat's (1997) parent teachers talked for, on average, 4 hours each. Researchers may be reluctant to say that so much time is involved for fear of putting people off. In any case, given that so much depends on the relationship that is developed and on the loquacity of the informant, it is not easy to tell with any accuracy before the interviews start, how long they are going to take. Furthermore, when initial contact with potential informants is made by letter or over the telephone, it may not seem appropriate or be possible to go into detail. Perhaps the best and most honest policy is simply to explain the nature of the work and that it can stretch over a considerable period, and leave it at that, giving the informant the assurance that they can quit at any time.

A similar question about how much to reveal, concerns the potential consequences of reflecting on and talking about one's life to an interested yet dispassionate listener. Undoubtedly, there are some similarities between Rogerian counselling and life history interviewing, in that interviewers, like counsellors, listen, reflect back, ask questions which encourage further reflection, and are non-judgemental. Both are also often dealing with intimate aspects of life. However, researchers are not (usually) counsellors: they are researching, not practising therapy (see Butt et al. 1992; Goodson 1992a). Yet, these characteristics of the approach can have implications for researchers and informants, and, occasionally, being involved in life history research can have life-changing effects. However, given that such outcomes are not common, it may be acceptable not to raise the possibility of anything of this kind happening to any particular informant. Also, these things are not predictable (or not predictable to researchers who initially are unlikely to be aware of events in an informant's life which may make them prone to radical life change) so, again, talking about it may be unacceptably preempting the issue. What is important is that, before they start work, researchers should have thought about the possibilities, should know that some informants may take advantage of the therapeutic potential of life history interviews, and should have considered their basic human responsibilities to other people (see Goodson 1992c: 245–8; Measor and Sikes 1992: 226). They need to be emotionally sensitive and intelligent and should exercise caution. Ethical questions and issues arising from relationships between researchers and informants are dealt with in detail in Chapter 6.

When the research has an essentially collaborative nature and involves informants as co-researchers, perhaps when a key focus of the project is professional and personal development, then exactly what is required of them has to be spelt out. Everyone has a notion of what research is, of what researchers want and expect, and of what research 'subjects' do. Often, this notion is based on ideas associated with 'traditional' research within the modernist paradigm. If informants come to a project with this notion colouring their expectations and responses, then misunderstandings can arise. Most researchers, particularly those who use interviewing, are used to informants saying something along the lines of, 'I don't know if this is relevant', or 'I'm not sure that this is the sort of answer you're looking for'. Responses of this kind reveal the influence that informants can inadvertently have on data through their eagerness to please. Clarity is, therefore, of the essence.

It is a good idea to give informants a written document to which they can refer, setting down expectations, 'rules', clauses and so on. If there is to be any deviation from this initial agreement, then the onus is on the researcher to negotiate the change. Such a document might cover the following areas:

1 Confidentiality and anonymity: the researcher should be clear about who is going to listen to tape recordings, have access to interview transcripts and other types of data and so on. They should explain how they are going to disguise, anonymize or otherwise protect the identity of informants. An approach which often proves popular is giving people the opportunity to choose their own pseudonym.
2 Anything about 'work' the researcher would like the informant to do, such as keeping a diary or writing accounts of particular experiences.
3 'Ownership' of any tapes and transcripts.
4 The informant's 'rights' to change, comment on, contribute to analysis and the eventual presentation of findings.
5 Where and when interviews will take place.
6 Contact numbers and addresses.

Strategies for collecting data

Interview-conversations

A one-to-one interview-conversation between informant and researcher is perhaps the most commonly used strategy for collecting life history data

(Goodson (2001) has referred to this as a 'grounded conversation'). Definitions of research interviews usually put the emphasis on their being conversations with the *purpose* of eliciting the information that the researcher wants (see, for example, Denscombe 1984; Powney and Watts 1987: vii; Robson 1993: 228–9; Fontana and Frey 1994), and various strategies and techniques are advocated for achieving this aim. Most of these strategies and techniques are concerned with establishing and maintaining a positive and trusting relationship between interviewer and informant, which takes us back to what we said at the start of the chapter about the importance of personal dynamics in life history work. Thus, researchers are advised to share their own experiences and perceptions (Oakley 1981), and to establish common ground through the clothes they wear, the interests they profess, the company they are seen to keep, the language they use and how they present themselves. In subsequent chapters we consider the ethics of manipulating relationships in order to get 'good' data, as well as look at epistemological issues around the 'truth' and validity of the accounts that people give in a research context.

Our general preference is for relatively unstructured, informal, conversation-type encounters. Of course, much depends on the particular focus of the research in general and, specifically, on the topics to be covered in a particular session, but – and this is a key characteristic of the approach – a researcher can never know for certain which experiences have been influential and relevant in a particular sphere of life, for sometimes connections are apparent only to the individual concerned. Conversely, it may be that events, experiences or personal characteristics, which the researcher expects to have been important, are not seen in the same way by the informant. Too tight a structure and schedule, and relevant information may be lost or, alternatively, may be given disproportionate emphasis by the researcher. 'On one level, perhaps, life historians have to accept that people tell the story that they, for whatever reason, want to tell to the person who is listening' (Sikes *et al.* 1996: 51).

Informants also respond variously to different approaches. Some prefer to be given detailed prompts, whereas others are quite happy to take their cue from key words or phrases.

Group work

The intensity and intimacy that is usually involved in life history research means that the study is generally carried out by the researcher and an informant working together. On occasion, group work can be used either as an additional strand of a project and perhaps focusing on a specific area, or with a collaborative and/or developmental aim.

Much depends upon the relationships between the various individuals who constitute a specific group and there is no way in which a researcher convening a group can know how the dynamics will work on any particular occasion. It may be that people are more likely to be frank and open with people that they do not know than they are with friends or colleagues. Equally, it is possible that a group who share a common experience will take a great deal of shared understanding for granted and will, therefore, leave out significant, or useful, explanatory details. Researchers have to try to consider the range of eventualities as thoroughly as possible.

If the relationships and consequent dynamics are conducive, group work can be very productive, in that accounts given by one person may jog others' memories about similar or contrasting experiences or perceptions. Having a number of people from different backgrounds and with different perceptions can mean that a wider range of questions is asked than if the researcher had been working alone.

The work of Frika Haug and her colleagues (1999) on collective memory work is especially important as a model for life history workers. Frika *et al.* have developed this memory work in collective settings as a way of investigating feminist topics, especially female sexualization. The use of these techniques in educational settings is long overdue, but as yet little work has been undertaken. A valuable exception are the Australian studies undertaken by Fitzclarence (1991). He has employed collective memory work as a strategy in involving student teachers in understanding the patterns of authority as they undertake the transition from the role of student to that of fully fledged teacher.

Pat Sikes and Barry Troyna (1991) used a group approach in their life history work which investigated student teachers' experiences and perceptions of schooling. The students first worked in triads, alternating the roles of interviewer, informant and recorder, and then came together for a full group (containing up to 30 participants) discussion. This was a particularly productive use of the approach because group members' experiences of schooling were so diverse. For example, between them, they had attended a vast range of types of school in a variety of countries. They were of different ages and belonged to different socioeconomic, ethnic and religious groups, and all of these differences were reflected in their perceptions, experiences, assumptions and expectations. Not only did the group-work have benefits for the researchers, it also contributed to the professional development of the student teachers, broadening their awareness and challenging their taken-for-granted understandings.

Group-work may also have a part to play in 'prosopographical' research. Prosopography is collective life history which aims to investigate 'common background characteristics of a group of actors in history by means of a collective study of their lives' (Stone 1987: 45). Since prosopographical research is historical, its sources are, primarily, documentary, but there may be occasions when oral evidence can be collected and group discussions could be useful.

Time-lines

A useful way to start life history research is by inviting respondents to construct a time-line of key events in their life with, if appropriate, an emphasis on those experiences which relate to any focus the project may have. This can be done prior to the interview and is useful in prompting memories and concentrating attention. The time-line can then be used as a structure for interviews, and to alert the researcher to experiences or phases of life which it might be productive to explore. Time-lines can be developed and expanded as the research progresses: alternatively they could be used just for their prompting value.

The sort of information that time-lines could touch on includes:

- Place and date of birth.
- Family background, birthplace and date.
- Parents' occupations during the informant's life; general character and interests.
- Brothers' and sisters' place and date of birth; occupations or school location; general character and interests.
- Extended family; occupations and character.
- Informant's childhood: description of home and general discussion of experiences.
- Community and context: character and general status and 'feel'.
- Education, preschool experience, school experience: courses taken, subjects favoured, credentials achieved; general character of school experience; peer relations; teachers; 'good' and 'bad' experiences.
- Occupation, general work history, changes of job, types of school, types of position.
- Marriage and own family: dates and locations.
- Other interests and pursuits.
- Future ambitions and aspirations.

(For a more detailed definition of life history time-lines, see Goodson 2001.)

Journals, diaries and other personal writings

Journals or diaries kept by informants can be an extremely rich, although not unproblematical, source of data. As Woods notes:

> why should somebody keep a diary? Hardly ever, I suspect, to preserve an objective view of facts. More likely it is to be for reasons like personal satisfaction in wishing to remember interesting events that have brought pleasure; or as a kind of celebration of self in annotating one's deeds, lest one forget; or as an apologia; or a kind of therapy in working one's way through a series of events that have brought personal diminishment, pain or embarrassment; or with a view to later publication and

public view. So one needs to know the basis on which the diary has been compiled.

(Woods 1986: 107–8)

Researchers using a life history approach are unlikely to be seeking an objective account but, acutely conscious of the need to contextualize and to know 'the basis' on which diaries are written, addressing the sorts of concerns Woods raises will probably be built into the research design. Similarly, such researchers are likely to interrogate and take an analytical approach to the language that informants use in both their written and oral accounts. And if they are not, then they should be.

In most cases, though, having access to diaries and journals will be a bonus, unless, that is, the researcher uses them as a primary source of data and asks informants to keep them for the duration of the project. In their 1991 study which focused on the socialization of new teachers, Bullough *et al.* used journals as one strand of their year-long case study approach. Unfortunately, but perhaps not surprisingly:

> early on in the year a problem surfaced with the journals . . . perhaps not trusting us, the teachers wrote the journals for us, and not for themselves . . . *another problem was* not all of the teachers continued throughout the year to keep up their writing. Indeed, two of the teachers found journal writing to be a source of increased anxiety and frustration and by mid-year had stopped writing all together. The other teachers found in journal writing a useful means for thinking about and making sense of their experience and faithfully maintained them.

(Bullough *et al.* 1991: 15)

Journal writing is clearly an activity which some people take to more easily than others. Some find it an extremely useful device for personal and professional reflection and development (cf. Holly 1989; Weiner and Rosenwald 1993); others quite the opposite. In their ongoing research, Judith Everington and Pat Sikes asked religious education students to keep journals and had a similar response to that experienced by Robert Bullough and his colleagues. In the first year of their study, whilst their informants were taking their Post-Graduate Certificate of Education qualification, Everington and Sikes were able to build written assignments into the course which they also used as data. Some of these assignments were assessed and, to meet accreditation requirements, had to take a relatively traditional academic format. The potential influence that these factors had on both the content and style of what was written had to be taken into consideration when it came to analysis.

As well as making use of journals and diaries as data sources, researchers are well advised to keep their own research diary, recording such things as who has been seen, what has been read, trains of thought, hunches and so on. Not only is a document of this kind useful for providing practical and factual information, it can also help with analysis and interpretation, in that it can jog memory and indicate patterns and trends which might have been lost if confined to the mind.

Using documents

Documents of various kinds, including syllabi, prospectuses, school reports, agenda, memos, letters, publicity material, school magazines, newspaper accounts and programmes of events, may cast further light on the life or lives being considered. Sometimes, researchers are able to collect relevant documents for themselves, but often they have to rely on informants to produce them. An interesting example of the use of supplementary documentation was provided by one of Pat's students who had undertaken a life history study of two 'delinquent' pupils. One of these pupils had attended an expensive independent girls' convent school. Publicity material and magazines produced by the school made it clear that girls were expected to conform to particular standards and types of lady-like behaviour. Correspondence between the school and the pupil's father, and her yearly reports during the time she was at the convent, documented the increasing mismatch between what the girl did and the school's expectations. The last straw was reached when the girl got very drunk whilst on a trip to the theatre. The final letter from the headteacher gave all the details and culminated in a request that the girl be withdrawn immediately.

Working with life history data

Recording data

Life history interviewing requires concentration. 'Listening beyond', picking up on clues and hints about what might be a productive line of enquiry, simply knowing what someone has said, all depend on the interviewer giving their total attention to the conversation and the social situation generally. This means that most life historians prefer to use tape recorders rather than rely solely on notetaking. Inevitably, taping is not without its problems. Machines break down or have faults, batteries fail, power cuts happen, people speak softly and extraneous sounds make it difficult to hear clearly. Then there is human error of various kinds. Most researchers have had the experience of forgetting to switch the machine on to record. For this reason, and also in order to provide an aide-memoire it is good practice to make some brief notes as well.

Researchers also need to consider the extent to which using a tape recorder influences the nature and content of what informants say. Some people may be inhibited by the knowledge that their words could 'come back to haunt them', and there are those who find it extremely difficult to speak fluently in the presence of a tape recorder. Often, in the course of recorded interview-conversations, people will ask for the machine to be switched off while they talk about a 'sensitive' issue or make comments about a particular person. Then there are those exchanges which take place before or after the interview has started. Thus, researchers frequently hear things relating to their project which are not part of their formally, or officially, collected data. This raises the question of what one should do with such information. If an informant has said something off the record and, what is more, has made it clear that they do not want their words to be attributable to them, then ethically the researcher should not ignore the request.

It can be argued that using a tape recorder introduces an element of artificiality into the situation. However, unless research, of whatever type, is undertaken covertly – an unacceptable approach for life history work – it is bound to be 'artificial'. Researchers and informants alike come into the research situation with certain expectations and preconceptions. These may include that interviews are recorded and that researchers can be trusted to use recordings responsibly. In our experience, the benefits of taping usually far outweigh any drawbacks, and most informants are, or become, reasonably comfortable with its use.

It is important to be aware that a recording only captures what is said, it cannot be a perfect, total and faithful representation of an interview, and even video recordings can only ever be partial.

Although, in our view, tape recording is to be recommended, there may be times when it is not possible. In these cases, the onus is on the researcher to make it clear that they are not working directly from the informant's words.

Transcribing

Having made a recording, the next stage is usually to make a written summary or complete transcript. This stage is time consuming and can be expensive in terms of transcription costs. There is no doubt that doing your own transcribing enables you to become familiar with the data. It can also aid analysis in that ideas and themes can emerge or be developed as a consequence of repetitive listening and intimate engagement with the data. However, even if someone else does the transcription, researchers should listen to the tape and follow the script to ensure that there are as few errors as possible. Such close listening is important because intent and meaning are conveyed as much through how things are said as through the actual words that are used. Annotations concerning tone of voice (and, if they can be remembered, or if a note has been made, body language and gestures) can add considerably to subsequent readings and interpretations.

We referred above to 'summary transcripts'. Rather than taking down every word, summary transcripts, as their name suggests, summarize what is said, using key words and phrases. It is important that a note is made of whereabouts on the tape particular things are said in order to facilitate verbatim transcription, if required, at a later date. Playback should, therefore, always be on a machine with a counter (this is a specification to bear in mind when buying new equipment). Making a summary transcript is, inevitably, analytical because it involves making decisions about how particular utterances are classified. Researchers should ensure that they note enough of what was said to enable them to make alternative interpretations if appropriate.

Analysis

Traditionally, following the positivistic paradigm of research, analysis of evidence took place at a particular stage of the research process: namely, after all the evidence had been collected and processed, in whatever form and by whatever means. This timing was to avoid the introduction of any contaminating bias. The extent to which neutrality of this kind is possible, or even desirable, is debatable (does/can anyone ever embark on any social research completely free of expectations or assumptions?), and life historians tend to the view that analysis begins as soon as they start working with an informant. Interview-conversations are not tightly structured and researchers will take opportunities to check out ideas, themes and thoughts as they proceed.

Analysis is about making sense of, or interpreting, the information and evidence that the researcher has decided to consider as data. This usually involves fitting the evidence and information into a framework of some kind. This framework may take the form of classifications, categories, models, typologies or concepts. The nature and origins of the framework and the extent to which it can be demonstrated that the evidence does actually fit and, thereby, the explanation holds, has been the central, the defining, research task. In the next chapter, we go on to consider epistemological questions of interpretation which focus on the relationship of life history accounts to the lives they represent. At this point, though, we do want to note that what constitutes a framework can be variously interpreted and, therefore, that it is up to the researcher to be explicit about their particular position. In itself, any story or life narrative is a more-or-less structured and ordered framework, regardless of whether it is someone relating their own life or a researcher retelling other people's (albeit through their own frame). In our view, the following observation applies to all parties involved in any narrative enterprise:

> Narratives select the elements of the telling to confer meaning on prior events – events that may not have had such meaning at the time. This is

a narrative transposition of Kirkegaard's famous statement that we live life forwards but understand it backwards. In understanding ourselves, we choose those facets of our experience that lead to the present and remain our life story coherent. Only from a hermeneutic position are we poised to study the genesis and revision of people making sense of themselves.

Narrative models of knowing are models of process *in process* . . . personal narratives describe the road to the present and point the way to the future. But the as-yet-unwritten future cannot be identified with the emerging plot and so the narrative is revised.

(Josselson 1995: 35)

Increasing awareness of researcher reflectivity and reflexivity means that more people take the view that interpretations/explanations/analyses are, inevitably, coloured and shaped by a range of influences, not least of which is the background, interests, in short, the biography, of the researcher. It is for this reason that some commentators have gone as far as suggesting that 'research biographies' should be compulsory because they provide readers with more evidence by which to evaluate research accounts (see Ball 1990, and various authors in Denzin and Lincoln 1994a). Indeed, since the 1980s, it has become common practice for qualitative researchers in general to 'write themselves into' their research, on the grounds that personal, background information will enhance the rigour of their work by making potential biases explicit (see, for example, Atkinson 1990). Whether or not it actually can do this is open to question (see Troyna 1994). In some cases there may be an element of what Mary Maynard (1993: 329) describes as 'vanity ethnography', that is when a researcher tells their story in a desire for self-publicity as much as, or more than, to support their work. It may also sometimes be true that, as Cotterill and Letherby (1993) suggest, some researchers do it in the hope that introducing a personal element will protect them from criticism. In life history work, where informants' lives are revealed, perhaps it is only 'fair' that researchers' lives are too – at least, in so far as what is told is really relevant to the project in question. Then, there is also the issue of actually and explicitly giving voice to the researcher themself which is, in effect, a further acknowledgement of the 'polyvocality of social life' (Coffey 1999: 118; see also Ellis and Bochner 2000). It would, perhaps, be inconsistent to fail to acknowledge that the researcher's voice is there among all others, especially if claims are made for the egalitarian broadcasting properties of the approach.

Analysis using computer programs

In recent years, an increasing number of computer programs (for example Atlas-ti, Ethnograph, Kwalitan, Nud.ist) which analyse qualitative data have become available. We shall do no more than refer to their existence and note that there is considerable controversy over the extent to which they can aid analysis, as distinct from their obvious capabilities when it comes to the storage and retrieval of data (for further discussion see Denscombe 1998: 218–22; Blaxter *et al.* 1999: 132–6; Miller 2000: 150–3).

The way in which researchers go about analysing evidence is, in itself, influenced by the epistemological and philosophical position they take. Whether they use analytic induction, constant comparative method, grounded theory, varieties of content or discourse analysis, thematic field analysis or some other approach, it is important that researchers are explicit about their practices and their reasons for them.

Respondent validation

Peter Woods (1996: 40) defines respondent validation as 'insiders confirming the correctness of analysis'. Yvonna Lincoln and Egon Guba (1985) argue that the standard for qualitative work is reached if informants find researchers' interpretations of their perceptions, experiences, or whatever it is that is being investigated, credible. However, as Norman Denzin (1970) has pointed out, it is not always that straightforward because informants might not like the interpretation or, if it is couched in specialist language, they may not recognize or understand it. Bev Skeggs, for example, reports that when she passed draft chapters and articles on to informants involved in one project she worked on, the most common response was, 'Can't understand a bloody word it says' (Skeggs 1994: 86).

Since life history work is so often collaborative, with researcher and informant seeking meanings and explanations together, respondent validation may well be built into the research design. If it is not, it is usually a good idea to ask informants what they think about any analyses or written accounts. However, researchers should bear in mind that, sometimes, informants do not expect or even want to be involved in any way other than by being interviewed. Researchers may find that, having passed transcripts and papers on to informants for their comments, they hear no more. On following up, they are likely to find that lack of time, or acceptance of the researcher's 'specialist' position is the usual reason given for non-response.

Researchers should also consider what they would do if informants disagree or ask for alterations. In some cases, the researcher may believe such changes to be appropriate, but in others they may not. What happens then? One way forward may be publication with a note to the effect that the informant(s) took a different view.

Data presentation

When all the relevant data have been analysed, the researcher is faced with the question of how to present their findings. (In Chapter 3, we look in more detail at some of the epistemological issues associated with turning a life story into a life history and in crafting a representation of informants' experiences and perceptions, but here we concentrate on practicalities.) So much depends upon the nature, scope and focus of any particular project, and on the type of presentation, its purpose, and the audience for whom it is intended. If it constitutes work to be submitted for a qualification (for example an assessed undergraduate project, a masters or doctoral dissertation), then there are likely to be official requirements and criteria, as well as conventional expectations to be met, and it is important for the student researcher to be clear about these.

When using data from interviews, and when the aim is to represent and reflect as closely as possible what an informant said, a key question tends to be how much direct quotation to use. Any synthesis or rewording by the researcher is a step away from the original, even when it is simply a matter of leaving out the 'ums' and 'errs'. Then there is the issue of how far the informant's words are left to speak for themselves and how much commentary and analysis there should be. Whatever decisions are made, the researcher needs to be able to justify what they have done. Thus, in some circumstances, it may be possible to leave a verbatim transcript to stand entirely alone (or with a minimum of comment) and in others, not to include any reported speech.

Some degree of editing is usual and is generally undertaken in order to support the researcher's case. This raises the issue of what is left out and why it has been omitted: an issue that is pertinent to many types of research, not just life history.

On occasion, researchers have explicitly presented their data in a fictionalized form (see Banks and Banks 1998). They may have amalgamated accounts given by a number of informants (see, for example, Clough 1999), or drawn on their knowledge of particular social situations to create a composite character. In some ways, this device is similar to describing types and there may be strong reasons for doing it. Andrew Sparkes (1995), for instance, created Alex, a gay physical education teacher, because he was unable to find such an individual who was prepared to take part in his study which focused on the sexuality of PE teachers.

In conclusion

In this chapter we have looked at some of the practicalities of doing life history research. We do not believe that there is only one way of doing such work, and each specific project will have its own idiosyncratic needs and aspects. For this reason, we have focused on what we see as the major concerns of widespread applicability. Above all else, the decision to take a life history approach should not be made lightly. This is research that can have an emotional effect on all parties involved. Life historians have to take seriously their responsibilities to their informants and readers: only if this is done can the march through the ethical and methodological minefield be completed successfully.

3 | What have you got when you've got a life story? Epistemological considerations

Introduction

What have you got when you've got a life story? And what happens when you turn it into a life history? What are the connections between a life story as told, the life that it concerns as lived, 'reality', and written accounts of life history research? These questions are in essence philosophical questions about the relationship between epistemology and methodology, between what knowledge is considered to be and the means by which it is obtained, recognized and deemed to relate to 'truth' (see Griffiths 1998: 35).

Traditionally, the goal of research has been to acquire knowledge which leads to understanding and truth or, more specifically, to the fixed immutable truth about whatever it is that is being investigated. Such a view of research is problematical for life historians since their primary aim is to explore how individuals or groups of people who share specific characteristics, personally and subjectively experience, make sense of, and account for the things that happen to them.

Life historians come in a variety of shades and flavours. They are not, inevitably, postmodernists, poststructuralists, feminists or relativists. However, we would be surprised if anyone who used the approach did not subscribe to the epistemological view that 'the social world is an interpreted world' (Altheide and Johnson 1994: 489), and that different interpreters who have had different life experiences are likely to make different interpretations which will, therefore, result in the description of different realities. Indeed, it is hard to imagine that anyone would even consider using life history if they did not have some sympathy with the concept of multiple realities and did not, therefore, see informants and researchers as being each engaged in interpreting the world from their own various perspectives.

This view has obvious implications for the nature and content of the life stories that informants tell and the life histories that researchers, often in collaboration with informants, construct and present in written format. Clearly, neither a life story nor a life history is anything other than a representation of the life they concern. The recognition and acceptance that it may never be possible to totally capture and faithfully recreate experience, is at the heart of the 'crises of representation and legitimation' occasioned by the problematization of the relationship between epistemology, methodology and the reporting of research (see Denzin and Lincoln 1994b: 9; Denzin 1997: 4–5; Goodson 2001). But, perhaps, the gap between 'reality' and representation does not matter or, rather, is not relevant. Tierney suggests that we should:

> refrain from the temptation of either placing our work in relation to traditions or offering a defensive response. I increase my capacity neither for understanding nor originality by a defensive posture. To seek new epistemological and methodological avenues demands that we chart new paths rather than constantly return to well-worn roads and point out that they will not take us where we want to go.
>
> (Tierney 1998: 68)

In this chapter, we want to focus on epistemological and methodological considerations relating to life history, from the perspectives of: (1) the life story teller – the informant – and (2) the life historian – the researcher. Since storytellers are often involved in historicizing their own story, and as the life historian is also involved in telling their story, differentiating the two is artificial. Nevertheless, for the purposes of organization and clarity within this text, we will do so, acknowledging that this is simply a stylistic device. Throughout the chapter, quotes from informants and life historians are used as illustrations.

Before proceeding, it is important to note that our concern here is with life stories and histories as 'data' in the context of research methodology (therefore, discussion of important associated themes such as self, time and memory will be cursory). It is the researcher who, regardless of approach, decides what constitutes, or what counts as data: a point that is, perhaps, particularly salient in the case of life stories and histories. This is because we hold to the opinion that it is through the construction, telling and retelling of our personal stories, to ourself and to others, that we attempt to make sense of our lives and give them meaning. In other words, personal narratives have a status as personal, as well as research, data. As Rapport (1999: 4) puts it, personal 'narrative is a means by which individuals existentially apprehend their own lives' (see also, Polkinghorne 1988; Bruner 1990). Margaret Attwood has her character Grace make this point eloquently when she writes:

> when you are in the middle of a story it isn't a story at all, but only a confusion; a dark roaring, a blindness, a wreckage of shattered glass

and splintered wood; like a house in a whirlwind, or else a boat crushed by the icebergs or swept over the rapids, and all aboard powerless to stop it. It's only afterwards that it becomes a story at all. When you are telling it to yourself or someone else.

(Attwood 1996: 298)

We tell stories about our life and our 'self', or rather our 'selves', as a sort of reflective interpretative device, with a view to understanding who and what we are and the things that happen to us. And yet, as Maroula Joannou (1995: 32) points out: 'although the self may only exist as a story that can be told about the self, what is told about the self is not always the same story, and much will depend on how it is told and by whom'. In any case, 'self' is a contested and controversial term. When we talk about our self, are we referring to our public, or private, or personal, or professional, or spiritual, or familial, or whatever, self? (See Mitchell and Weber 1999: 8.) Is it ever possible to present a comprehensive account? Whilst we may work hard to present ourself as having a unified coherent identity (because to fail to do this is to come across as mentally unstable), our view is that, at a very basic level, we are multi-self beings and it is incumbent upon life historians to be explicit about this when they are about the various aspects of their work.

Life history from the perspective of the life story teller

What is going on when someone tells their life story or, more usually, a part of their story, as an informant in life history research? Ken Plummer (1995: 34) suggests that, in essence what they are doing is turning themselves into 'socially organised biographical objects'. They are telling their story in a particular way for a particular purpose, guided by their understanding or conceptualization of the particular situation they are involved in, the self/identity/impression/image they want to present, and their assessment of how hearers will respond. This happens in all social situations, not just in the context of research. It is worth noting though, that the opportunity that being involved in life history research provides to tell your life story, to craft a narrative that links together events, experiences and perceptions, is the explicit opportunity to create an identity (see Ricoeur 1980). In some ways, this is a unique experience:

> I don't know what you got out of it in that I don't know if I said the right sort of things but I really appreciated taking part in this. I don't think I'd ever sat down, seriously and thought about me, about who I am and what I am and how my life's worked out. It was fascinating to uncover the different influences and consequences and what have you. I certainly came away with plenty of food for thought. And I know it sounds all 60s, but I'd say I've got a better sense of who I am through

the experience. I'd recommend it to anyone! (*Sylvia, 'Parents Who Teach' project.*)

(Sikes 1997)

There's a way in which, having been put in that situation, you think about who you are and how you come over to other people. It's a chance to, sort of articulate yourself. To describe yourself and when you've done it, it gives you more confidence to be that person – if you know what I mean. I suppose you could make up a total pack of lies, and maybe no one is 100% honest but for me, what I said was what I'd like to be and I keep striving! (*Stephen, 'RE Teachers' project.*)

As social beings we constantly story our lives, but in different ways and using different words in order to fit specific contexts, purposes and audiences. Consider, for example, what we might say and how we might say it in the following scenarios when we may well be talking about more-or-less the same sorts of thing:

1 At the doctor's, when giving an account of our lifestyle for medical and health reasons.
2 Telling someone we have met for the first time at a party about ourself.
3 In a job interview when giving an account of our career history.
4 When our children ask about when we were young.
5 To a lover at the start of what we hope will be a serious and enduring affair.
6 To a life historian researching how and why people go into teaching.

Not only might our own stories alter depending on the context and what we judge to be appropriate, politic or useful, they differ from other people's stories as a result of the unique combination of experiences we have had and the knowledge we have amassed as we go through life. Life, as we live it, is a processual matter rather than a product. As Woods (1999: 4) notes: 'social life is ongoing, developing, fluctuating, becoming. It never arrives or ends'. Nor can there ever be the definitive story about a life or an aspect of a life. Alternative interpretations are always possible, depending on the perspective, values and motivations of the storyteller. When it is our own life that we are talking about, we may change our interpretations and our stories as we remember or forget different details and as we assume (for whatever reasons) different perspectives and acquire new information. All stories, all biographies, can be told from various perspectives and in a range of styles. For example, let us take stories about the first day at school, since these could easily be relevant in a life history context:

I was really looking forward to going to school, I thought it was going to be wonderful. I'd heard my cousins' stories about school and I wanted to be a 'big girl' too. My mum had taken me to visit the school and the headmistress, Mrs Barnes, and I'd read to her and been excited by the water table and the sand tray and when anyone asked if I was looking forward to school, I said yes. On the first day my mum dressed me in a new plaid kilt and a pink blouse that she'd made 'for school', there wasn't a uniform in those days. I had a little purse on a string round my neck with a hankie in it. We walked down the village and stood outside the school gate. My name was called and me and mum walked under the arch and into the cloakroom. I took my coat off. Mrs Kirby the teacher showed me my peg with a teddy bear picture above it then took my hand and led me into the classroom and sat me down at a table with paper and crayons, asked me to draw a picture and then pinned a pink card badge with my name on it, onto my blouse. I noticed that some children had blue ones and I wished I had because blue was my favourite colour. Then I realised mum had gone. I had never, ever, been away from her in my life. Never, ever. I said, 'I want to go to my mummy'. 'She'll be here at dinnertime', said Mrs Kirby. I wanted her now. I wanted her so badly it hurt. I had never felt so unhappy in my entire life. I started to cry and I couldn't stop. Mrs Kirby was busy bringing more new children into the classroom. I thought she wouldn't notice if I left so I went out to the cloakroom got my coat and was just walking through the door when Mrs Kirby came up behind, took me by the arm and said, 'Come back into the classroom Katherine. You can't go home yet. Your mummy will be here at dinnertime'. Well I cried until dinnertime. I cried, with relief when I saw mum, cried all the way home, all through dinner and then when my dad said he was going to take me back to school on his bike on his way to work, I cried even louder. I had a tantrum. I kicked and screamed and flailed about. My mum started to cry then. Dad got me out the house and on to the seat on the crossbar on his bike. I wept as we cycled through the village. When we got to the school he lifted me off the bike, took my hand, said, 'Be a brave girl', took me into the classroom and left me, still crying. I cried all that week. I missed my mum so much. I felt totally betrayed. (*Kate.*)

It was horrible. I came home from taking Kate to school and sat and howled. I cried all the morning. I didn't get anything done because I missed her so much. What was I going to do with my life now, while she was at school? And when she came home at dinnertime and got so upset it was even worse. Her dad was upset because she was so distressed. It was awful. (*Kate's mum*)

I have never had a child in all my years of teaching who cried as much as she did. I shall never forget what a sad little girl she was. It quite upset me because usually they cry for a bit and then they're all right but she carried on for a whole week. She just didn't stop. She was heart-broken and I was beginning to wonder what to do because of the effect it was having on the rest of the class. And you have to remember that in those days I had 40 children to cope with! (*Mrs Kirby*)

I remember Kate in the first week because she cried all the time. I thought she was a real mardy-bum, a mummy's girl. I was quite naughty because she said, 'My mummy says I don't have to go to school on Saturday and Sunday'. And I said 'Oh yes you do. Your mum is wrong'. I did it just to make her cry more! Dear me. Sorry! (*Kate's friend*)

In this example, the accounts all contain the same basic story of a child's first days at school, but from differing perspectives, reflecting different concerns and priorities. Furthermore, whilst these accounts are attempts to remember the story as it would have been told at the time, years after the event, some of the people involved would give interpretations which were, at least, slightly different. For instance, Kate now sees her experiences as the consequence of her mother's 'failure' to adequately prepare her for independence. She attributes this failure to the fact that she was an only child who, quite wrongly, in her view, was the 'be all and end all' of her mother's existence. As a result of what happened to her she determined to make sure that her own children would be used to being away from her right from their earliest days. On another theme, she also pointed out that she had noticed the stereotypical colour differentiation of the girls (pink) and the boys (blue). Without wishing to pre-empt the next section of the chapter, it is worth noting that a life historian researching issues to do with gender would probably emphasize this aspect of the story, whereas someone whose focus was starting school may mention it but would not necessarily give it the same degree of prominence within their account.

Different interpretations over time are almost inevitable. This is because our experiences and the professional and personal knowledge we may have gained as parents, teachers, playgroup leaders, child psychologists, sociologists, lunchtime supervisors, life historians, or whatever, inform the sense we make of the events. They may lead us to feel that we have a more accurate and comprehensive picture than we had at the age of 5. Nevertheless, whilst the child's story may be partial and the adult the child has become may well wish to revise it, unless it is consciously and deliberately a lie, it is an authentic account of an experience. We agree with Clandinin and Connelly's claim that:

stories are the closest we can come to experience as we and others tell of our experience. A story has a sense of being full, a sense of coming out of a personal and social history ... Experience ... is the stories people live. People live stories, and in the telling of them reaffirm them, modify them, and create new ones.

(Clandinin and Connelly 1994: 415)

And then there is the question of memory. In one sense, all stories are memories as all memories are stories. Even Proustian recollections of sensation, sparked by taste, smell, touch, emotional feeling, whatever, are usually translated into words and the past is brought into the present through narrative. Why we remember some things and forget others is, perhaps, always to do with how whatever it is we are remembering fits, or has fitted, into one of our stories. As Hampl (1996: 207) notes: 'we only store in memory images of value. The value may be lost over the passage of time . . . but that's the implacable judgement of feeling: this we say somewhere deep within us, is something I am hanging on to'. (See Mitchell and Weber 1999: 46–73, for a useful discussion on memory).

Being asked to tell one's story as part of a life history research project brings the relationship between the story, the life as lived, and methodology into acute focus. As we noted in Chapter 2, people have particular notions of what it means to be involved in research (see also Denscombe 1984). These notions influence what they tell and how they tell it, and their ideas about the information that they consider they should make available to the researcher. There is no getting away from this, however much researchers may try to ensure that they have been as open and explicit about their enterprise and their aims as they possibly can be. This point is particularly salient for life history researchers because, as Bruner notes:

> the-story-of-a-life as told to a particular person is in some sense a joint product of the teller and the told. Selves, whatever metaphysical stand one takes about the 'reality', can only be revealed in a transaction between a teller and a told, and as Mishler reminds us, whatever topic one approaches by interviewing must be evaluated in the light of that transaction.
>
> (Bruner 1990: 124)

Life historians do frequently emphasize to their informants and in their published accounts that the construction of a life history from a life story is a joint creation. Frequently, some form of explicit researcher/informant analytical cooperation is even incorporated in their research design. It is also important to be aware of, and to acknowledge, the extent to which the relating of the life story is itself a collaborative activity with implications for the nature and content of the story which emerges and, in some ways, for the future lives we live and our understandings of them. As Munro notes:

> life history interviews are themselves texts designed to not only give shape to some feature of experience but ultimately to create a self. As Bakhtin (1981) suggests, there is an intimate connection between the project of language and the project of selfhood; they both exist in order to mean. There is no identity outside narrative. Events or selves, in order to exist, must be encoded as story elements. Narrative, as Ricoeur

(1974) reminds us, imposes on the events of the past a form that in themselves they do not really have.

(Munro 1998: 6)

Thus, when someone tells their story to a life historian, they can be seen to be actively involved in constructing a version of their story and of their life: generally a version which is linear and relatively neat and tidy in a way that real life, or rather, lived experience, never is (see Roberts 1999).

We tell our stories using the narrative forms available to us within our cultures (see Passerini 1987: 28; Goodson 1995: 95; Plummer 1995: 21). These forms act as templates, both for the telling of the story and in the way they impose a structure on our experiences and perceptions. As Erben (1998b: 13) argues, lives have to be understood as lived within time and time is experienced according to narrative. In its commonest form, narrative structure generally has a beginning, a middle and an end, and events are usually depicted as proceeding consecutively and logically. Sometimes this is what has happened, but often things have not been quite so straightforward. Many of the things which happen to us result from complex interrelationships and serendipitous occurrences. In choosing to relate one particular storyline we are, in effect, closing off other, alternative ones. Goodson (1995) has written about the way in which prioritizing one story over another can be used to further political ends: it can have a similar effect in the personal sphere too as people may choose to emphasize certain experiences in order to support the impression they wish to project, the representation they want to make.

Then there is the question of gaps. What is left out can be as significant and as telling as what is included – provided that researchers are able to discover omissions, which is by no means always possible (see Sikes 2000a). Nor is it always the case that in leaving things out informants are deliberately seeking to mislead. On the contrary, they are often concerned and anxious to ensure that the story they tell is relevant. They ask, 'Is this relevant?', or comment, 'I don't know if this is the sort of thing you're interested in'. In effect, what they are doing is seeking confirmation that they are telling the 'right' version of their story, the version that they believe the researcher wants to hear (and, as we discuss in the next section of this chapter, the researcher is then implicated in deciding which version to privilege).

Accepting that life is not neat and tidy, logical, consequential and consistent, perhaps, in these postmodern days, presents researchers with less of a dilemma than was previously the case. As Linda Wagner-Martin (1998: 93) notes: 'post-modern readers reject oversimplification – preferring an unfinished narrative or one with gaps in its construction to the deceit of the contrived finish'. But that is postmodern readers, who perhaps belong to an esoteric minority. Most people, in telling their lives will try to impose some order, however spurious, because they are concerned to make sense of the things that have happened in order to avoid anoesis and anomie ('anoesis' refers to sensations or emotions that we do not understand, and 'anomie' to hopelessness and the loss of any sense of purpose or belief). People also often feel that everyone else's life is neat and tidy and logical, partly because this is how they tend to be described – which takes us back to the issue of narrative forms, what is available to us and how such forms can end up shaping perceptions and experiences.

> I always feel that everyone else has got things sussed out and that I'm the only one who isn't. You listen to people talking and they've got all their lives sorted. They're going to get married, and they do, then they're going to have the requisite number of children at the times that they want and everything's going to be fine. I thought it would be like that for me and it wasn't. I got married all right but the children didn't come. I felt a failure. A total bloody failure. And there were my sisters and sisters-in-law producing left, right and centre and I couldn't even get pregnant. I was a failure as a person. It wasn't until after we'd adopted our daughter that I learnt that one of Brian's sisters had had a number of miscarriages and that one of my brothers' wife had been taking Clomiphen [a 'fertility' drug] for a couple of years. We hadn't been told those stories but it would have helped me a great deal to have heard them. (*Nicola, 'Parents Who Teach' project*)
>
> (Sikes 1997)

In a life history context, our facility with language, our general fluency and articulacy and our ability to dramatize and tell a story determine how 'good' an informant we are. To a considerable extent they also determine the 'success' of the identities we construct. Wittgenstein (1953) commented to the effect that the limits of our language are the limits of our world, and it is certainly the case that the vocabulary we possess enables us to present ourselves as more or less sophisticated, interesting, reflective, intelligent, spiritual (and so on) people, as it also enables us to interpret and make sense of our experiences with more or less precision and complexity. Whilst there is a personal dimension to fluency, and some people are simply better at telling stories and talking about themselves than are others, the language and discourses we have access to depend upon the social contexts we experience and how we are socially positioned. As Usher notes:

> [people] can only represent themselves in language by creating a 'literary' rather than a 'literal' figure that dis-figures or de-faces as much as it figures ... Discourses and positioning shape what and how we experience the world . . . we are constituted in language and positioned differently depending on the discursive practices of gender, race, class, ethnicity and other marks of difference.
>
> (Usher 1998: 19–20)

Frequently, it is these 'marks of difference' that life historians are looking out for when they are analysing life stories. In other words, they are seeking 'common verbal patterns' (Casey 1993: 23), or patterns of discourse, which are taken as indicators of whatever it is they are suggesting marks out, or is characteristic of, their informants. Here, once again, the issue of the nature of the relationship between epistemology, methodology and reported accounts of research looms large. To repeat the questions we raised at the start of this chapter: What have you got when you've got a life story? And what happens when you turn it into a life history? What are the connections between a life story as told, the life that it concerns as lived, 'reality', and written accounts of life history research? Given what we have said in this chapter about the ways in which people conceptualize research and their involvement in it, about how we use pre-existing storylines or narrative forms and about how our language has a great deal to do with where we are socially located, there are no categorical answers. When someone tells their story as part of a life history research project they are involved in a creative act, irrespective of how committed they are to telling the 'truth', or telling it as it was. Rather than attempting to make unrealistic claims for representing 'reality', life historians should simply acknowledge what they are able to do with the stories they use as data: namely, offer an interpretation through their writing and spell out the influences that may have coloured both the teller's story and their interpretation of it.

Life history from the perspective of the life historian

If life story tellers are involved in creating and crafting a story when they take part in life history research, then to what extent are life historians engaged in creative activity when they design, undertake and eventually write up their research? Our basic answer is, to a considerable degree – as are all researchers using any other approach. Fundamentally, research is about furthering understanding, increasing the universal sum of knowledge, and making 'better' sense of whatever it is that is being studied. Thus, researchers are seeking to interpret and then re-present an aspect of the world, whether that be of the physical, objective world or of subjective, lived experience.

As noted earlier, we do have considerable sympathy with Clough's (1992: 2) view that, 'all factual representations of reality, even statistical representations, are narratively constructed', and, therefore, creatively constructed. What are the implications of acknowledging that the research process in general, and writing up in particular, is in essence creative? And, how can life historians justify their position and differentiate themselves from straightforwardly avowed writers of fiction? This is not to suggest any qualitative evaluation, but rather to signal that researchers and writers of fiction tend to have different motives and agendas for their writings (see Baronne 1995: 65).

In this section, we try to begin to answer these sorts of question. This needs to be done because, unfairly in our view, life historians and other qualitative researchers are criticized for 'subjectivity' in a way that those working within the positivist and modernist traditions are not. Whilst these criticisms continue to be made, newcomers to the field need to have some 'ammunition' with which to defend their corner. We shall concentrate on the processes by which researchers make their interpretations and, specifically, communicate their 'findings' to others through what they write: in other words, on what life historians do with the life stories they collect; on how they go about using these stories to make a re-presentation of 'reality'. Of course, if life history is a collaborative venture, or for personal and professional development, then the key audience is the informant. In this case, the communication between researcher and informant is crucial but, perhaps because of the intimate and immediate relationship between both parties, there is more space for negotiation of meaning, for discussion of the relationship between epistemology and methodology, and more room for questioning the researcher as to their meaning and intention.

We have already referred to the so-called crisis of representation. Denzin argues that:

> A single but complex issue defines the representational crisis. It involves the assumption that much, if not all, qualitative and ethnographic writing is a narrative production, structured by a logic that separates writer, text and subject matter . . . Any social text can be analysed in terms of its treatment of four paired terms: (a) the 'real' and its representation in the text, (b) the text and the author, (c) lived experience and its textual representations, and, (d) the subject and his or her intentional meanings. The text presumes that there is a world out there (the real) that can be captured by a 'knowing' author through the careful transcription (and analysis) of field materials (interviews, notes, etc.). The author becomes the mirror to the world under analysis. This reflected world then represents the subject's experiences through a complex textual apparatus. The subject is a textual construction because the real flesh and blood person is always translated into either an analytic subject as a social type or a textual subject who speaks from the author's pages.
>
> (Denzin 1997: 4–5)

(The reader and their interpretations and understandings are of great importance too, but Denzin is himself writing from that position.) Those who acknowledge that there are problems inherent in any attempts to offer a 'definitive' version of reality are acutely conscious of the ways in which differential social positioning and life experience militate against the possibility of there being a single, literal writing or reading of any text. Baronne quotes Witcombe who, in endorsing Barthe's announcement that 'the author' is dead, chooses to redefine herself as a writer having previously considered that she was an author and states that, 'as a writer [unlike an author] I do not have an agenda [in the sense of a list of things to accomplish]. But like everyone else I write from a political position' (quoted in Baronne 1995: 65).

It is possible to take the view that this is all just so much semantic posturing. Of course, writers have 'an agenda'. And authors 'create' – but then, so do writers. Perhaps the nature of what they *claim* to create is what is of paramount importance. In this view, the onus is on the writer/author/researcher to be as explicit as they can. After all, a key 'test' for assessing whether or not qualitative research writing is representational of 'real' life has been the extent to which it achieves what has been called verisimilitude (Bruner 1986): that is, how far it seems to be true, how far people who have personal experience of the focus of the research regard it to be likely, or the extent to which 'experts' in the field consider theories, conclusions etc., to be plausible. Yet, as Todorov (1977: 83) has noted, there are multiple verisimilitudes. It is also possible for accounts to have verisimilitude but be 'untrue' (Sikes 2000a), or to lack verisimilitude and be 'true' (Lincoln and Denzin 1994: 578). After all, as they say, truth is stranger than fiction. And yet, perhaps somewhat confusingly in the context of this discussion, verisimilitude is exactly what most fictional writers are seeking to achieve. Consider what Virginia Woolf has to say about successful fictional writing:

> The writer must get into touch with his reader by putting before him something which he recognises, which, therefore, stimulates his imagination, and makes him willing to co-operate in the far more difficult business of intimacy. And it is of the highest importance that this common meeting place should be reached easily, almost instinctively, in the dark, with one's eyes shut.
>
> (Woolf 1992)

Fundamentally, if writers/authors of 'fiction' or 'fact' are to communicate effectively with their readers there has to be some point of imaginative contact, some 'common meeting place'. Even science fiction and fantasy writing takes account of this. Thus, we can feel fear with Bilbo Baggins when he encounters Gollum even though we are not Hobbits (and nor, as far as we know, are there any such creatures as Hobbits) and even though we have never been to Middle Earth (which does not exist), because Tolkein draws on emotions and experiences common to humans. Experimental writers in all genres and disciplines ignore this at their peril, and as I write I am reminded of a couplet from an otherwise forgotten poem:

'What is conceivable can happen too',
Said Wittgenstein who had not dreamt of you.

That the imaginable does tend to be possible is central to arguments supporting the use of 'critical fictions' for educational and professional development purposes (see Banks and Banks 1998; Bridges 1999; Clough 1999). Critical fictions frequently take the form of life and case histories and provide examples and scenarios which people can use to consider how they would respond to and deal with such situations.

Baronne (1995: 64–5) proposes 'that inevitably associated with the act of writing is the attitude of *persuasiveness*'. Indeed, why should anyone write anything if they do not have some message to pass on (even at the level of the shopping list to remind oneself of what to buy)? There is nothing inherently sinister, Machiavellian, unscientific, unobjective, or necessarily partisan about this. Thus, not only do life historians re-present the life stories they are told, they do so within the context of their own frames of reference and the particular stories that they wish to tell via their use of what informants say. And they have made the decision that a life history approach, inclusive of the writing/reporting styles associated with it, is the most appropriate one for telling their story, for making their interpretation, their re-presentation, for getting their message across. This, yet again, highlights the relationship between epistemology and methodology. An example of this relationship concerns the origins of Pat's work, *Parents Who Teach* (Sikes 1997). Basically, she was surprised to find how her world-view, her personal and professional perceptions and experiences changed when she had children:

> Although this surprised me it should not really have done. The reason for this is that some years earlier I had worked on a research project which used biographical methods to study secondary school teachers' experiences and perceptions of teaching (Sikes, Measor and Woods, 1985). A colleague, Lynda Measor, and I had, between us, interviewed 40 teachers of various ages and at different career stages. Around three-quarters of these teachers were parents and all of them had mentioned the ways in which they believed they had changed, with regard to their work, once they had had their children. I knew about the 'phenomenon' I was experiencing, I had talked to teachers about it, I had even written about it but in some ways it did not register. The impact of parenthood had only been a tiny part of the work we were doing and we had not explored it in any detail or given it any special significance. I now think that this was because I was guilty of what Michelle Fine describes as 'Othering' (1994), that is, of seeing the teachers I was working with as separate, distinct and different from me. Now that I had become a mother and was aware of how significant that experience was for my professional life, the process of 'othering' was interrupted and I could hear, with clarity, what those teachers had been trying to tell me. I needed to go back and listen more carefully to what parent teachers had to say, not least in an attempt to better understand my own experiences.
>
> I subsequently set up a research project which focused on teachers' perceptions of the ways in which parenthood had influenced all aspects of their professional lives.
>
> (Sikes 1997: 10)

The story that Pat went on to tell was all about this. As Ann Oakley (1979: 4) has noted: 'academic research projects bear an intimate relationship to the researcher's life . . . personal dramas provoke ideas that generate books and research projects'. Most people's preference among research topics is likely to be for ones which have meaning to and interest for them, and this meaning and interest generally stems from something in their own lives. Of course, for a variety of reasons, researchers do sometimes end up working on projects designed by other people. Even then, even when working within specific parameters, we would suggest that people tend to draw on their own interests and experiences. The accounts that they write reflect this and, once again, issues of gaps and omissions, of prioritizing and politics loom large. As before, our advice is to be as reflective and reflexive as possible and to make this explicit to readers. Indeed, with regard to acknowledging the part that our research can play in our lives, we go along with Coffey's uncompromising position that:

> Emotional connectedness to the processes and practices of fieldwork, to analysis and writing, is normal and appropriate. It should be acknowledged, reflected upon and seen as a fundamental feature of well-executed research. Having no emotional connection to the research endeavor, setting or people is indicative of a poorly executed project.
>
> (Coffey 1999: 158–9)

An issue related to 'whose story' is being told, concerns the use of informants' words to tell their own story. Life historians commonly do make extensive use of quotations and transcripts from interviews and, in Chapter 2, we discussed questions relating to editing and selection. It is important to bear in mind that any decisions regarding how much or how little editing there should be are taken with regard to the story that the researcher wishes to tell. In a paper about consensual sexual relationships between teachers and students, Pat presented life history interview data with minimal editing because she was concerned that readers should see the issue from the perspective of her informants, rather than from the normative, censorious position. In the following extract, readers can reflect on how the use of different words in accompanying commentary, could have put a very different slant on the interpretation/re-presentation of Hillary and Matthew's story:

Matthew and Hillary: A Tragedy?

Hillary was 17, in the lower sixth, studying for A levels, when Matthew, aged 35, took up a part-time appointment at her school. The couple met when Matthew started supervising one of Hillary's timetabled English private study periods. They were instantly attracted to each other.

'I thought he was gorgeous. It was love at first sight. He had lovely blue eyes and a gentle voice and he was really interesting to talk to and, not to beat about the bush, I wanted to go to bed with him.' (*Hillary*)

'She was beautiful. She walked through the door and I immediately fell in love with her. She had long blonde hair and I was always a sucker for that, but she was so sparky and alert and full of enthusiasm for life and, so it quickly seemed, for me too. I couldn't believe that she felt like that about me but I never dreamt anything could come of it. She was too perfect.' (*Matthew*)

There were around 15 students in the group, most of whom resented having their private study overseen. Matthew sympathised with their point of view and with the agreement of the headteacher, gave them permission to go off and work in the library. Eventually, after four or five weeks, Hillary was the only student who turned up. During their first session alone together they talked about one of the books on the syllabus, Thomas Hardy's *Tess of the D'Urbevilles*.

'I was dreadful. I said that I thought Tess was a silly cow, that I far preferred Alec and I started giving all these hints about how sexually experienced I was. He clearly found it difficult but I was remorseless. I wanted him and I'd made up my mind to have him. I remember I asked him if he was married or had a girlfriend – he wasn't and didn't – where he lived, what he did at weekends, where he went and so on. I was sitting on the desk and I got closer and closer and I thought yes, you are interested. When the bell rang for the end of the period I leant forward and gave him a kiss on the cheek and said "See you on Saturday".' (*Hillary*)

'I was really quite frightened but excited at the same time. She was really coming on to me. There was no mistake about what she was after. And when she kissed me I was so totally non-plussed that it took me some time to realise that she'd said she'd see me on Saturday. Anyway, Saturday afternoon came and I was sitting reading – every minute of that afternoon is engraved on my mind even though it was the best part of 30 years ago – when the doorbell rang.' (*Matthew*)

'I'd come into town on the bus and all the way I kept repeating a sort of litany in my head, "Let him be in, let him be in". And he came to the door – "you were so surprised weren't you?" ' (*Hillary*)

'Yes, I'd never really expected her to appear, so I was a bit diffident, but of course I invited her in and offered her a glass of wine and we sat down on the sofa and talked about books and things and then – "shall I tell her?" ' (*Matthew*)

'Yeah.' (*Hillary*)

'She started kissing me and I responded and then, God, it was as if heaven had come to earth she said, "Take me to bed Matthew." ' (*Matthew*)

'Yes, and I didn't know until earlier this year that up to that point you were a virgin. "You must have been terrified." ' (*Hillary*)

'I was!' (*Matthew*)

Matthew had never experienced such depths of emotion for anyone before:

'I'd always run away from women but she wouldn't let me go and I couldn't let her go. I hadn't known that it was possible to love anyone like I loved her and the most wonderful thing was that she said she felt the same about me. I was obsessed, besotted. I wrote her poems and letters and spent every lunchtime with her. It became clear to everyone that we were having a relationship. And I didn't care, but I overdid it.' (*Matthew*)

'I loved him so totally and it was clear that he felt the same about me but I was 17 and he was 35 and, so, I thought, totally sophisticated, that I was convinced that he'd become disillusioned with me and I couldn't bear the thought of that. I thought I'd die if he stopped loving me – you know how you are at that age.' (*Hillary*)

After a few weeks, senior staff started to get alarmed by the indiscreet behaviour of the couple and informed Hillary's parents about the relationship. She had kept it secret because she 'knew they wouldn't approve' of her going out with a man so much older than her who was a teacher into the bargain. There were angry scenes and meetings at school:

'It was dreadful. Everyone seemed to be making what was so wonderful, so sordid. They wouldn't listen and we've since realised they told me some dreadful lies about Matthew, implying that he was a paedophile with a history of preying on young girls. I just couldn't cope with the pressure they were putting on me. It was dreadful at home and dreadful at school and the counsellor started coming out to talk to me at home in the evenings. I got so confused and I just didn't know what to believe, I was only 17 after all and nowhere near as mature as I liked to think. Then, as I've said, I was frightened that he'd fall out of love with me. If he'd asked me to marry him it might have been different.' (*Hillary*)

'But I couldn't because I'd been told that I was making you unhappy and ought to get out of your life before I ruined it and leave you alone and anyway I was frightened that you'd say No. It was a dreadful, dreadful time.' (*Matthew*)

The outcome was that Hillary ended the relationship and Matthew left the school. The following year she went away to college in another part of the country. Thus the 'scandal' was contained within the school community, although it was fear of it spreading that had led to the senior staff's actions. And it has to be noted that these actions very nearly had fatal consequences: Matthew seriously contemplated suicide, seeing no point to life without Hillary, whilst she attributed the anorexia that she suffered from for 7 years, to her misery at being parted from the man she loved.

On the basis of the story as presented here, readers might conclude that this was an immature pair who were a danger to each other, themselves, and anyone else they may have come into contact with. They do not see it that way because they believe that, without the intervention of the school and Hillary's parents, there is a good chance that their relationship would have endured and that neither of them would have experienced so much mental anguish and illness. As it was, eventually, they each married other people, had children, and led relatively successful professional lives. But, with a twist that seems straight out of a novel (Vikram Seth's, 1999, *An Equal Music*, perhaps), almost 29 years after they parted, they came across each other through work. By now Matthew was 61 and Hillary 43. They were both delighted and horrified to meet again: delighted because each of them had never got over their separation and they were glad that it was ended; horrified because they found that they still felt exactly the same about each other but now had partners and families they didn't feel able to abandon. Whatever the morals of the situation, when they spoke to me they were maintaining an affair which they intended to continue as long as they could.

Reflecting on the past, they did not believe that Matthew, as a teacher, had exploited Hillary, as a pupil. They did, however, feel that the way in which the authorities had interfered with their relationship was unwarranted, impacting as it had, on the rest of their lives and, ultimately, on the lives of their spouses and children.

(Sikes 2000b)

Continuing with the theme of persuasion, Baronne writes:

since an important intention of the writer is indeed the intention to persuade, then the corresponding stance of the storyreader is understandably one of *vigilance* against abuse of authorial power. Writers and readers of narrative can also occasionally share a mutual aim in their textual activity. This is the aim of securing power for the characters whose stories they choose to craft and remake. Pursuance of this common goal can lead to dialogue in which mistrustful, writer-versus-reader antagonisms are temporarily suspended, as all agents conspire within an emancipatory moment.

(Baronne 1995: 65)

Acknowledging that research reporting tends to be persuasive does not necessarily imply that writers do not adopt a critical approach to what they write. It is our experience that most life historians, whilst being keen to argue their particular line, are extremely concerned that their work be taken seriously. This means that they do seek to ensure that their research and writing are undertaken with regard to 'criteria for adequacy'. The important point is that the criteria should be appropriate to the nature of life history work. Hatch and Wisniewski offer a review of suggested criteria for quality life history work and note that there is a need to go 'beyond the standardized notions of reliability, validity and generalizability' (Hatch and Wisniewski 1995: 128–9; see also Rosie 1993; Sikes 2000a). Having said that, when working from transcripts of life stories, life historians seem to be in general agreement that: 'we cannot write just anything we wish, . . . interpretations, however tentative must be disciplined by data, and . . . we must proceed cautiously and carefully before proclaiming a plot' (Bullough 1998: 29) and that, whilst:

> imagination is the vehicle the researcher employs to aid recognition of significant moments in the data, to relate these to each other and to the overall lives of the subjects under study . . . at all points, however, the researcher is required to fix imagination in empirical sources – it cannot be allowed free rein and take unwarranted liberties with the lives of subjects. The fact that biographical research findings are imaginative constructions does not mean that they need to be fictitious.
>
> (Erben 1998b: 10)

This brings us back to the fundamental difference between life stories and life histories, which was discussed in Chapter 1.

In conclusion

In this chapter we have considered aspects of the relationship between methodology and epistemology. In particular, we have focused on the relationship between, (1) the stories informants tell of their lives as lived, and (2) the life stories as data and life historians' re-presentations of them as research accounts. In neither case can the stories be seen as the lives themselves but, we argue, they are perhaps as close as it is possible to get. Social positioning influences the stories we are able, and that we wish, to tell. This, in itself, is useful analytical information for life historians.

4 | Studying teachers' life histories and professional practice

Introduction

Whilst studies of teachers' lives and careers are informative and fascinating in their own right, they can play an important part in furthering understanding of a wide range of topics to do with education and schooling. This is because, as Goodson (1981: 69) has written, 'in understanding something so intensely personal as teaching, it is critical we know about the person the teacher is'.

Teaching is an interactive, relationship-based activity *par excellence*. Given that teachers play the key role in interpreting, mediating and realizing what goes on in educational institutions, their values, motivations and understandings have considerable influence on professional practices of all kinds. Life history methodology, uniquely perhaps, enables the exploration, the tracing and tracking of this influence through the way in which it attempts to take an holistic approach to individuals in the various contexts (for example social, political, economic, religious, geographical, temporal) they inhabit. Life history work also has considerable potential as a strategy for personal and professional development, thus furthering an individual's own self-understanding. In this chapter we look, albeit cursorily, at some of the ways in which studying the teacher's life history can contribute to the understanding and, thereby, the development of professional practice.

Our starting points

We both became convinced, early on in our careers, that investigations focusing on such areas as pedagogy, curriculum development, school administration, leadership and organization could all be enhanced by the inclusion of a life history element. The ways in which we came to this view are, we think, instructive as to the general argument for such forms of study.

For Pat, illumination dawned inexorably in the course of her doctoral research that looked at how mid-career teachers were perceiving and experiencing reduced prospects of promotion owing to falling rolls (Sikes 1986). Initially, the main concern was to find out whether, how, and in what ways disappointed career expectations affected teacher motivation and performance. The study was quite large for one person to undertake but, following the traditional line that large samples were necessary and that generalizability was essential for validity, Pat pressed ahead, initially undaunted.

A multi-method approach was adopted. Structured 36-item questionnaires were eventually returned by 1200 respondents, a week of ethnographic fieldwork was undertaken in each of 25 secondary schools throughout England and Wales, and 120 interviews, lasting an average of three-quarters of an hour, were conducted and transcribed. Analysis resulted in patterns, tendencies, categories, models and a typology of attitudes to career ('Normal Norman', 'Pissed Off Pete', 'Restless Ron', 'Coasting Colin', and so on). Generalizations could be made but these came to seem irrelevant in the light of the individual life histories, the idiosyncratic stories that led to teachers appearing, at any particular time, to fit into one group or another. This point was brought home when, on a Thursday, Pat interviewed a young man who was very concerned to locate the questionnaire he had completed on the Tuesday. On the intervening Wednesday, the man had both been promoted and learnt that his wife was expecting their first child. He was worried about 'spoiling' the research because of how his attitude and circumstances had changed over 48 hours. But that is life. And reducing life to manageable categories, however tentatively presented, falls far short of representing the shifting, complex, personal reasons why people feel and behave as they do. In Britain, the governmental endorsement, and consequent financial support, is for educational research which, 'demonstrates conclusively that if teachers change their practice from x to y there will be significant and enduring improvement in teaching and learning' (Hargreaves 1996: 5). Thus, 'we are not interested in worthless correlations based on small samples from which it is impossible to draw generalisable conclusions' (Blunkett 2000: 20). On one level, such efficiency is clearly desirable, but on another, and given the personal, interactive, relationship-based nature of education, generalizable conclusions may well have limited impact on individuals' experiences of teaching and learning, schools and schooling (see Faris' comment on Stouffer's experiment in Chapter 1).

Ivor similarly realized that life histories were important with regard to professional practice and development during a period of intensive curriculum development, whilst teaching in a comprehensive school in the Midlands. Working together in a team with a number of university-based researchers on a Ford Foundation Project looking at teaching styles, it became obvious to him that to understand how innovation and change were being taken up, the focus needed to move from curriculum development towards teacher development. Writing later about this shift, Ivor and Rob Walker considered a teacher they had been studying, one 'Ron Fisher':

> involvement in innovation, for Ron at least, is not simply a question of technical involvement, but touches significant facets of his personal identity. This raises the question for the curriculum developer: what would a project look like if it explicitly set out to change the teachers rather than the curriculum? How would you design a project to appeal to the teacher as a person rather than the teacher as educator?
>
> (Goodson and Walker 1991: 71)

The understanding that teachers' life histories were important, grew out of intense involvement in professional development activities. In fact, re-capitulating on the belief that the link between professional development, professional practice and life history work was substantial, Ivor has looked into his own past in order to trace back his conviction that teachers' work and life histories were central to a reconceptualization of educational study and professional development:

> The first episode took place in the year of post-graduate certification when I was training to be a teacher. I returned to spend the day with a teacher at my secondary school who has been a major inspiration to me, a mentor. He was a radical Welshman. Academically brilliant, he had a BSc in economics and a PhD in history. He was open, humorous, engaging, stimulating – a superb and popular teacher.
>
> But he faced me with a paradox because when the school changed from a grammar school to a comprehensive, it was he who opposed all the curriculum reforms which sought to broaden the educational appeal of the school to wider social groups. He was implacably conservative and traditionalist on this and, so far as I know, only this issue. But he, it should be remembered, was a man who had personally visited the factory to which I had gone after leaving school early at fifteen. He had implored me to return to school. He had spoken then of his commitment to public schooling as an avenue to working class emancipation. He no doubt saw me, a badly behaved working class pupil, as some sort of test case. I knew personally then that he was very deeply concerned to keep working class pupils in school. So why did he oppose all those curriculum reforms which had that objective?
>
> During the day back visiting my old school, I continually probed him on this issue. At first he stonewalled, giving a series of essentially non-committal responses, but at the end of the day, in the pub, over a beer, he opened up. Yes, of course he was mainly concerned with disadvantaged pupils; yes, of course that's why he'd come to the factory to drag me back to school. Yes, he was politically radical and yes, he had always voted Labour. But, and here I quote:

you don't understand my relationship to the school and to teaching. My centre of gravity is not here at all. It's in the community, in the home – that's where I exist, that's where I put my effort now. For me the school is nine to five, I go through the motions.

In short, in the school he sought to minimise his commitment, he opposed any reform which dragged him into more work. His centre of gravity was elsewhere.

The point I'm making is that to understand teacher development and curriculum development, and to tailor it accordingly, we need to know a great deal more about teachers' priorities. We need in short to know more about teachers' lives.

The second episode began in the late 1970s. I was interested in some work on folk music being conducted at the University of Leeds. At the same time, I was exploring some themes for an ethnography conference that was coming up at St Hilda's in Oxford. The work of a folklorist Pegg suddenly opened up again the line of argument which I had been pondering since 1970. Pegg says:

The right to select lies not with the folklorist ('Sorry old chap, can't have that – it's not a folk song'), but with the singer. Today's collector must have no preconceptions. His job is to record a people's music, whether it is a traditional ballad or a hymn or a musical song or last week's pop hit!

With this basic attitude comes another revelation:

I began to realise that, for me, the people who sang the songs were more important than the songs themselves. The song is only a small part of the singer's life and the life was usually very fascinating. There is no way I felt I could understand the songs without knowing something about the life of the singer, which does not seem to apply in the case of most folklorists. They are quite happy to find material which fits into a preconceived canon and leave it at that. I had to know what people thought about the songs, what part they played in their lives and in the lives of the community.

(Goodson and Walker 1991)

A similar point is made by the folksong collector Robin Morton:

The opinion grew in me that it was *in* the singer that the song becomes relevant. Analyzing it in terms of motif, or rhyming structure, or minute variation becomes, in my view, sterile if the one who carries the particular song is forgotten. We have all met the scholar who can talk for hours in a very learned fashion about folksongs and folklore in general, without once mentioning the singer. Bad enough to forget the social context, but to ignore the individual context castrates the song. As I got to know the singers, so I got to know and understand their songs more fully.

(ibid. 1991)

The preoccupation with 'the singer, not the song' needs to be seriously tested in our studies of curriculum and schooling. What Pegg and Morton say about folklorists, and implicitly about the way their research is received by those they research, could be said also about most educational research.

(Goodson 1991: 35–6)

These personal reminiscences and episodes are presented, in part, to substantiate the link between the study of teachers' lives and issues of professional development and professional practice. Having said this, we are cognizant that life histories exist in an ambiguous, intersecting location between the personal and the professional (Goodson and Hargreaves 1996; Goodson 2001).

We sometimes think that, like cigarettes, life histories should come with a warning along the lines of: 'life histories can seriously impair your understanding' if they are poorly constructed and badly used. This is because life histories are such complex and often contradictory mechanisms. Much has to do with their location: they exist at the intersections and on the sites of our multifaceted struggles for selfhood and identity. By their very location, then, they are supremely suited to provide windows into the complexities of our social being. Life histories, then, must be treated with great care, but the rewards for social enquiry and for professional development can, nonetheless, be great.

Let us mention one or two contradictions that hint at the difficulties. In the current period of postmodern fragmentation, with traditions and established practices coming under threat, our struggles for identity face remarkably chaotic and disparate environments. The life history may serve in the face of a fragmentary existence as a site to re-establish some sense of unity and coherence. The more fragmentary our existence, the more unified our life stories may become. At this point, our life experience and our story of it may be almost oppositional. This relationship between life experience and life story will, we suspect, oscillate and alter during the life course and at different historical times.

Likewise, the social script of expectations, which each of us comes with into the world, creates different 'parts' for different people. For the rich white male, the social script written before birth (shall we say when 'his name is put down for Eton') may prove acceptable and will be lived and storied as planned. For those of other class, race and gender, the script that is written by society will be more oppressive, and the life may be lived as an attempt to deconstruct the social script.

Life stories then are contradictory mechanisms. For this reason, among others, we have developed a distinction between life stories and life histories. This does not resolve many of these issues, but seeks to wrestle with some of the factors at play. The life story is the story we narrate about the events of our lives. This story often refers mostly to the inner dialogue which we have called 'our reflexive project of selves'.

The life history is collaboratively constructed by a life story teller and life story interviewer/researcher. Therein, the aspiration is different from that of the life story. The aim is to 'locate' the life story as it operates in particular historical circumstances. A range of data is employed: documents, interviews with relevant others, theories, texts, even physical locations and buildings. These data are, so to speak, triangulated to locate the life story as a social phenomenon existing in historical time. The life history, then, aims to create a different story from that of the personal life story. In this story, the wider worlds of power and meaning are situations in which the life story is embedded. Without this, we posit, the life story is a limited perspective and a potentially dangerous data site, for as Samuel (1989: 23) has argued: 'History from below ... without some larger framework ... becomes a cul-de-sac and loses its subversive potential'.

Developing life history data can help in broadening our understanding of the teacher's professional work. The following section provides one example of how this pursuit of research data, comprising the teachers' whole life perspective on their work and practice, can transform our understandings. Not all such data provide such smooth transformation, as in this example: in some ways it all seems 'too neat'. But this example has been chosen precisely because it does show the power of life history work with unusual clarity.

Introducing computers into a teacher's life: issues of professional practice and development

In the late 1980s and early 1990s, the province of Ontario, Canada, went through a massive programme of investment to provide computers in school classrooms. A number of research projects were funded to examine and evaluate this initiative. Since then, Ivor has been working on one of the largest projects, to be reported in *Computer Wars* (Goodson *et al.* 2001).

The project team comprised a large group of research fellows and faculty members, covering a spectrum from the techno-fanatical to the Luddite-cynical. The example given here examines one teacher's response to the computers being introduced into his classroom as a vehicle for commentary on the methodological nuances of the study.

In the initial period of the research, the focus was mainly on classroom observation and technological orientation workshops. However, Goodson, the project coordinator, and Mangan ('interviewer' in the subsequent extracts), the senior research officer, were both concerned to broaden the focus away from an analysis of technological implementation. Goodson, a non-technical Luddite, and Mangan, a techno-enthusiast with sociological reservations, began to argue for a set of life history studies to search for a broader set of insights into the impact of computers on the teacher's life and work.

This broader focus led to a reformulation of how a teacher's response to computers was initially represented. The first data on Jim, a geography teacher, focused on his response to being invited to join the project and to the early orientation meeting:

> *Interviewer:* Um . . . so it wasn't explained to you how they happened to pick you or uh, why they landed on you rather than someone else in the department?
>
> *Jim:* No, I was just stopped – stopped in the hall by the principal and Pete. I didn't know Pete ahead of time, so . . . and it sounded good at the time, but I regretted after that I had done it, okay? Although I have some . . . non-regrets, too, because now I know a little bit about it, and I'm going to become involved, and I slacked off, mainly because – not mainly because – my department head is so involved in computers, so – and he got involved, so he took up the slack for me and he'll have to reteach me a lot of it.
>
> *Interviewer:* So, did you understand that the project would require a fair bit of in-service training when you first got involved?
>
> *Jim:* Oh, yes, yes, yes. I – I've had a sinking feeling that this was going to happen. But, uh, I went to the first number of meetings, but it did fall off after, okay? And it's – I must admit totally fallen off right now. So, I'm gonna have to pull myself up by the bootstraps and start again next fall.

Jim then, from the beginning, struck a note of reservation, 'that sinking feeling', which could sometimes express itself as 'resistance':

> *Interviewer:* That's interesting, 'cause one of the other teachers recently said they found that meeting a little intimidating with all those honchos there, and uh, but you didn't feel that way about it?
>
> *Jim:* No, no. I try not to let people intimidate me . . . [interviewer laughs] . . . if at all possible. I was there as a volunteer, I wasn't being paid. They wouldn't – there's no threat on my life – I mean, they're not gonna cut me off or anything. So they can say, 'You're doing a crappy job'. That's fine, okay, uh . . . Give me a pat on the back, but it's not gonna change my salary, it's not gonna change my position, it's you know, I'm the one involved, so, you know, I don't find people intimidating me or . . . [telephone is ringing].

Research team members' initial responses to Jim were not unlike the way in which teachers come to stereotype and sort out the children in their class on the first few days. Working with lots of people, you tend to create short-hand categories and stereotypes – they are inadequate, and you know that, but they can become ossified: 'first impressions stick'.

One first impression of Jim was that he was a 'resister'. Knowing Goodson's Luddite predilections, the research team kept noting, 'we think we've found you a resister', 'Hey, Jim's the Luddite you've been looking for'. Although these were jokes, they expressed serious aspects of the truth: Goodson did have reservations about computers and seeing a teacher express these through his reservations and resistances confirmed these feelings. Sometimes Jim expressed this quite directly:

Interviewer: Yeah. Well, I guess where that might tie back in with computer use is . . . one thing that some teachers express concern about is that using computers is an equalizing and unif. . . an imposition of a more uniform curriculum. In other words, you can't alter the computer curriculum to the same extent that you could play around with your own lesson plans and your own teaching materials and so forth. Do you see that as a danger in any way? Or . . .?

Jim: No, because . . . not in my lifetime. The computer isn't going to take my place.

Interviewer: No?

Jim: No way!

Interviewer: You don't think it will limit your freedom either though?

Jim: It'll . . . it'll limit your freedom if you become a slave to it and enter . . . everything centres around the computer, then, yes, your freedom is gone. But, as far as I'm concerned, my lack of using it, is pretty indicative right now that maybe I'm not going to let somebody else . . . something else interfere with me. No, I've always thought of it as a super supplement to other things that go on in the classroom, other types of lessons. Okay, to build up a basis of kids being able to use it for the lab work. Where they're on their own and they have to interpret or maybe they have to draw or they have to extrapolate something. Because I want to get back to the spreadsheet. It looks so neat. So I did a lot of work on that. It's not going to take my place. At least, not in seven years, okay.

At other times he expressed a more ambivalent view: seeing the problems for his own work life and then focusing on the rationale from the point of view of his students:

Vicky: Uh . . . You said that the teaching aids and AV [audio visual] material and things like that have changed. How do you feel computers fit in to that?

Jim: Well, it's the next change that I've got to swallow. As I've admitted to you before, I'm still kind of frightened of it because I haven't gotten into the swing of it yet. And it's going to start very soon and I'm crossing my fingers that I'm not going to fall on my face. If I fall on my face I'm still going to live, so I'm not going to worry about it. But it's absolutely so useful a tool that it's gotta come, and I've gotta just break my back and get away from maybe old-fashioned things that I've been doing and get on with the new, because uh . . . all the kids coming out of high school should have some degree of expertise in computers. And I'm not going to preach about geography being so important that it's absolutely necessary, but just the application of computers for a lot of jobs, for the simple reason that geography is not going to be something they're going to be working with for the rest of their lives.

From the team members' point of view, then, Jim was a resister who expressed some ambivalence. In his actions though, Jim was clear: again and again, from early 1989, he was 'just too busy' to introduce computers into his classroom or to go to the computer laboratory with his class. He said he was 'frightened' of falling 'on my face', and his actions confirmed this. But he promised that in the summer of 1989 he would buy his own computer and develop some 'stuff' for his class. In the event, he did nothing and our fieldnotes confirm the growing conviction that Jim was not going to 'buy into' computers:

> Jim didn't seem particularly thrilled to see us. Despite his avowals at the end of last term, he quickly confessed that he had spent his entire summer either at the cottage or travelling in Eastern Canada. No mention of summer computer projects. I told him that I was now the principal investigator responsible for geography [his subject] and that, as such, I would be willing to help him sort out some applications for his classes. He indicated that he would try to develop some stuff soon, with the help of Steve and myself. However, he would be coaching soccer again this year, and he would be absent the third week of September, on a tour of Northern Ontario sponsored by the Ontario Mining Association.
>
> Similar to last year, Jim already has a lot of 'extra' things scheduled for this year. He said that he was one of a group of teachers selected to attend a weeklong session on Mining in Ontario, to be held in northern Ontario from September 23–30. This means that he will be missing an entire week of school already, and his class will have a substitute teacher. In addition to this, he will still be coaching junior boys' soccer

this year. He said he didn't plan to, but after finishing in first place last year, he just couldn't say no!

Then, in the summer of 1990:

> We now seem to have established good rapport with almost everyone in the project. Jim may be the one exception. He seems wary of us, although I think he likes us personally. The other day, at the Brock Art show, he commented that 'I avoid everything to do with computers'. Nothing ruins a relationship like guilt, and I think he feels guilty around us. He feels he has not fulfilled some obligation he made to the project, and to us as part of that project. Even so, he always seems friendly towards us personally.

If, for the research team, Jim was 'our resister', to his colleagues, he was a 'beached whale', 'a burnt out case' – clapped out and ready to retire and they very directly expressed the belief that he would 'never' take up computers:

> Steve then turned to me with what he called a 'simple question'. He wanted to know what was going to happen to geography in the project. Jim hasn't used the lab yet and, as far as Steve is concerned, is never going to use it. He said that he would tell us that he is going to use it, but he'll come up with excuse after excuse and never use it. He knows, because he's been through it with him before, with no success. He is concerned that Jim will be representing all geographers in our reports. I assured him that that would not be so, but he felt uncomfortable with the situation. He said that he didn't want to push us into anything, but it might be a good idea to visit his classes as well. I told him what Jim told us of his plans for this year, but that he has just been too busy so far. He said that it was true, but Jim will always be too busy with other things to find time to use the computer . . .
>
> There were people in geography that were already involved in dealing with computers but not on this level. Not on a level where we can actually teach kids using the computers, because they don't have them. And this was an opportunity to actually have enough computers to really use them in the classroom. So I wanted geography involved. It didn't have to be me particularly. But I'd already tried to get Jim involved with the Commodore and, I mean, I'm not talking about a one-shot try. We tried over and over, every professional development day we had there for a while, we had at least something involving, you know, getting them hands-on a computer. And nothing happened and I knew that that was likely to happen again.

Both the research team and the other geography teacher came ultimately to agree that Jim was representative of a type:

Interviewer: Yeah, well it's, I mean for one thing we did want the project to be an effort in moving into some new areas like, you say, not just science, math and accounting. So that was one of the reasons we wanted to have geography and some of the other subjects. And, actually, whatever the history behind it, I'm sort of glad that we've got Jim because I think one of the things that happens too often in these evaluation projects is that you only get really enthusiastic and sometimes people with a great deal of background knowledge, as your own.

Steve: Yes, that's right.

Interviewer: And it creates a sort of artificial situation. I mean, one thing that I think is going to be useful to our evaluation is to try to figure out what the sort of sources of resistance or reluctance for people like Jim are, because I don't think that you can expect everybody to embrace computer use in schools with open arms.

Steve: Nope. He certainly proved that. No, I agree. As a research tool you've to look at the whole spectrum and he's certainly part of that spectrum. There is no question about it. But at the same time if you were going to, you know, once you'd established that, there is an awful lot of information that came out of things that somebody who is *using* the computers could provide that he'll never be able to provide you with.

Interviewer: Right. Which is exactly why we wanted to get you more involved.

So, by now, the researchers and Jim's colleagues had more-or-less come to a consensus on Jim. In the fieldnotes, Mangan expressed it this way:

Although I do not want to attempt a psychoanalysis of Jim, the following factors seem to me to combine to account for his reluctance to get involved with computers:

* Personal insecurity: habits of methodical preparation; fear of being unable to completely master or control the material during a classroom presentation; inability to completely control the material presented by the programs.
* Established teaching patterns: related to above, his presentations seem very uniform, semester to semester. He has chosen certain teaching aids which he has used for up to twenty years without change: 'Socratic' style.
* Personal relationship with students: Jim likes to get to know them

personally; he jokes a lot with them, makes individual eye contact in every class; acts quite fatherly towards most of them.

- Individualised treatment: Jim has repeatedly affirmed his disinterest in marking programs, because he feels there are intangible considerations which must go into a student's final grade. He feels computers are too insensitive to the individual needs and circumstances of each student.

- Technophobia: and finally, Jim has repeatedly described himself as 'old-fashioned', by which he means not only that he uses old-fashioned teaching techniques, but that he is committed to a traditional concept of literacy. He emphasises the need to be able to write well and to deal with maps and written material. He may be suspicious that computers undermine that traditional literature culture.

And there, probably, matters would have stayed. However, by now, the team had undertaken and were transcribing Jim's life history interviews. These life history collaborations allowed them to see events in a crucially different way from more normal research observations and interviews. They provide 'grounded conversations' to explore issues deeply. Some of the burnt-out case hypothesis was actually brought up in these interviews:

Interviewer: I should probably know this from earlier interviews but it's slipped my mind. How close to retirement are you?

Jim: Seven years.

Interviewer: Seven years.

Jim: Well, five to seven years.

Interviewer: So it's not just around the corner.

Jim: No.

Interviewer: Because I mean, what I'm getting at there, is I wonder whether . . . I mean even from . . . if it were me, I think I might wonder about whether the investment in learning something as complex and as big as Computer Assisted Learning at this stage was going to pay off for me . . . in the few remaining years of my career. Do you think that's part of it, at all?

Jim: No.

Interviewer: No? You are still interested in new . . .

Jim: Seven years would be my ninety factor [making up the full pension allowance], okay. If I was totally fed-up or ill or something with the other . . . age fifty-five . . . with penalty, or it could go on a little bit longer. So . . . no, in terms of a fiscal investment I don't think so. I can't say my wife and I are poor, so it's not that.

Other matters emerged in the interviews. As well as turning fifty, Jim's father had just died and he was spending a lot of time visiting his ill mother.

VR: And do your parents still live in Windsor?

Jim: Uh . . . no, my uh . . . (long pause) . . . my father died about four years ago and my mother is in a nursing home right now.

VR: Nearby?

Jim: No, down by Blythe, not too far. It's only an hour and fifteen minutes away. So I see her, but uh . . . to tell you personally she's not in very good shape, right now, so . . .

VR: It makes it difficult.

Jim: Uh . . . We're expecting it, you know, her to die, okay, we all know what's happening and uh . . . she wants it that way so . . .

Hence, we began to get some sense of the way the trajectory of the project 'collided' with the trajectory of Jim's life. An alternative hypothesis was thereby generated. Maybe Jim was telling the truth when he said, as he kept saying, 'I'll get to it in the end'. This did seem, after all, a tough time in his life: burying his father, immersed in his mother's final illness, turning fifty. At another level, it began to seem almost heroic for Jim even to attempt a major new undertaking under such circumstances: his acceptance of all the blame seemed suddenly stoic.

Interviewer: I know you've got to go soon. Do you have any other comments about how the project's gone? Do you feel like you've gotten enough support from us at the Faculty?

Jim: Yep, yep. I just haven't taken advantage of you, that's all. So it's . . . it's only one person to lay the blame on and that's me. I have . . . it's down there, it's waiting to go . . . Steve is willing to help and I've been the oversized elephant with lead in my feet. So it's up to me. It's not your fault or Valerie's or Steve's or the school's or anybody else. It's me. So, we're going to start next week. We're going to make the time.

Quite suddenly, the fieldnotes change. In January 1991, for instance, Mangan wrote:

I should also note that, during my interview with Jim, he mentioned that it was his birthday, and that he was fifty-one, as of the day of the interview. This had the effect of retroactively explaining a lot of earlier stuff. I had just read an article by Tom Brokaw in *Esquire* about the trauma of turning fifty and it suddenly struck me that, all during the earlier parts of the research project, Jim had been approaching, or living through, the age of fifty. His comments about feeling tired, worn out, and old-fashioned suddenly leapt into sharp focus. His generally troubled and distracted air may have something to do with this. And, not least, the fact that he survived his fiftieth year, and that that particular crisis is now behind him, may have paved the way for him to finally move ahead with a challenging new project which he had been putting off for months.

Other explanations began to emerge:

> Steve then said something that may hold the key to Jim's reluctance to get involved: he said that Jim is a very well-prepared teacher, who always spends a great deal of time getting ready for each class. Steve said that Jim keeps careful records of previous lesson plans and exams, and consults them frequently. He has seen Jim completely replicate a handout for a class by re-writing it, even though it could be simply reproduced from the older documents.

Meanwhile, Jim had begun, in his own time, to take up computers – after two years of 'resistance' and as the project had in effect finished. A good job that the life history interviews had made the team stay with him.

> I started the day in the computer lab, where Jim was once again. While starting later than the others, he seems to be going full steam ahead with the computers. He has had both classes in three times already and has the lab booked for periods 1 and 5 (his two OAC [Ontario Academic Credit exams] classes) on the following dates: November 22, 23, 27, 29, 30 and December 3. He was busy printing copies of maps in the lab for use with upcoming projects.

The new sensitivities developed through life history conversations began to emerge in new accounts of the situation:

> Jim, having 'lost his virginity' with the computers, now cannot get enough. He has booked his classes into the lab for 6 of 8 days. To some extent, this appears to be an imitation of Steve's exercise for OAC students. However, I also believe it has to do with the whole rationale for Jim's reluctance to date. He did not want to use the computers just to do some sort of half-assed exercise; if he was going to use them, he wanted it to be a serious data analysis problem. He has now jumped in at the deep end and is doing a great deal with the system all at once. He is having problems, but coping with them pretty well.

Raising issues

In this chapter, we are trying to raise a number of issues with regard to life history and professional practice. Firstly, questions about the limits of existing research paradigms to illuminate professional practices. The conventional methods of research observation, structural interviews and surveys are often driven either by researcher perception or practitioner folklore. These are severely circumscribed methods because they fail to engage within the intersection between professional practices and the whole-life perspective of professional practitioners. Little attempt is made to explore professional life and work as intersecting with wider whole-life perspectives. One researcher on doctors explained:

> So much of the work on doctors sees their life only through a professional prism. If they were to see doctors' work, as primarily viewed, as 'an interesting hobby' for middle class men, so much would be viewed differently.
>
> (Douglas 1998: 4)

Professional work cannot and should not be divorced from the lives of professionals. As can be conclusively evidenced in the example provided, life history studies have the capacity to transform the content of analyses of professional practices. Once professional practice is located within a whole-life perspective, it has the capacity to *transform* our accounts and our understandings. The limits of conventional research and accounts are exposed. In so doing, research accounts can be dramatically reconceptualized and transformed.

Associated with the reworking of accounts is the issue of personal voice and perceptions, such vital issues when thinking about teachers' professional development. In the collaborative life history interview, a reciprocal sharing of views and perceptions takes place, although on a stratified and sedimented terrain. The professional practitioner is empowered to voice a wider range of concerns, and to do so as a dialogical exchange which can change both the nature of the account and the nature of consciousness (for both professional and researcher). Our collaborative dialogue has the potential to substantially rework our understandings of professional practice. Such collaboration can help our studies of professional practice and does so in ways that illuminate the intersection between life and work. This kind of collaboration is a relatively unexplored modality in studies seeking to reconceptualize understandings of professional practices.

These transformations of understanding are crucially relevant to how we rethink our professional development schemes. What the example of Jim shows is how narrow and misguided a 'technical fix' view of professional development can be. So much professional development work, for instance, a lot of national curricula preparatory work has proceeded by ignoring or denying the person that the teacher is. This issue is sidestepped by concentrating, as with computers, on techniques or content. By tailoring our professional development to a whole-life perspective, a different process can be conceptualized and undertaken. At the commonsensical level, we know professional development works only if it involves teacher development, that is personal development. And yet, in the conventional professional development strategy, the personal is usually ignored. By focusing more on the life and work of teachers, our strategies for professional development might be substantially improved. Professional development and personal development can be brought into a closer relationship and thereby work in harmony, as opposed to the more conventional model of division and denial.

There is another sense in which life history approaches can transform the professional paradigms of research. Much research creates a culture of expertise and privilege for the researcher, alongside a culture of silencing, appropriation and academic colonization for the researched. Life history seeks, not entirely successfully, to 'level the playing field'.

In some sense, the inequity that is structured into conventional research is destabilized. For the researched are, themselves, the experts about their own lives: nobody knows better than them the intricacies and intimacies of their life. The researcher, cast into the role of listener, assumes the initial role of learner. From this base, collaboration and analysis follow, but the flow of information and dialogue is partially monitored by those researched. The research trade is, therefore, different from the conventional model. But, with every kind of solution come new problems. Life history, whilst changing the terms of trade, sets new critical dilemmas (some of which we explore in Chapter 6). Not least, the access that may be granted to the intimate details of professional life has to be carefully managed in terms of more public reporting and publication. But also, the new research method sets up new inequities, re-establishes old inequities, and provides new potentialities for appropriation and colonization. Life history, then, as we have said, comes with no 'health' guarantees. By changing the terms of engagement, new possibilities can be glimpsed, explored and perhaps consolidated.

Life history as a strategy for personal professional development

We have focused so far on life history as a research methodology, an approach to collecting and analysing data and producing accounts to the end of furthering understanding about teachers' lives and careers, about professional practice, education, schools and schooling, and so on. We have noted the collaborative nature of the approach, the way in which the inform-ant is, in essence, a partner, a co-worker without whose cooperation and active involvement any study cannot proceed, but the emphasis has remained on the *research* endeavour. In this section, we consider, briefly, the potential that biographical work, and life history in particular, has for per-sonal and professional development.

Over the years, various people have written about the uses and benefits of auto/biographical work within initial and in-service teacher education (for example, Abbs 1974; Grumet 1981; Woods 1985; Aspinwall 1986; Woods and Sikes 1987; Holly 1989; Bullough *et al.* 1991; Butt *et al.* 1992; Sikes and Aspinwall 1992; Pinar 1994; Bullough 1998). Those who advocate auto/biographical strategies for professional development have identified and emphasized the following potential benefits.

1 *Benefits from engaging in self-reflection.* Here the emphasis is on the improved self-knowledge which can result from examining and reflecting on our lives, on understanding 'where we are coming from', and considering where the beliefs, values and experiences that we hold and have originate and how they have developed, and how our past might influence our present and our future. Life history demands an holistic approach and, therefore, forces us to think about the relationship between different aspects of our lives, and about the influence and impact that our different (social) selves might have for, and on, each other. So, for example, we can look at the ways in which religious background and beliefs might affect motivation to teach in the first place and then subsequently influence professional practice; or, at the ways in which becoming a parent might impact upon teachers' work, and vice versa, at how being a teacher might have implications for how people approach parenting (Sikes 1997). Self-awareness of this kind can enable informed development and change in perception, attitude and practice of all kinds (see Bullough *et al.* 1991; Bullough 1998; Butt *et al.* 1992).

2 *Benefits accruing from space to reflect.* Teaching is hectic work. Apart from the constant demands on their attention from students, colleagues and parents, teachers have to cope with the changes (relating to curriculum, assessment, administration, organization, and so on) imposed by governments and local boards. Taking some time to step back and examine and appraise what we are doing and why, frequently has positive consequences for practice and attitude (see Abbs 1974; Woods 1985; Aspinwall 1986; Holly 1989).

3 *Benefits from learning about schools and schooling, theory and lived experience.* Schools and schooling are a fundamental feature of western cultures and societies. Almost everybody attends schools, everybody knows what schools are like – or, rather, they know what their particular schools were like for them ('them' being specifically positioned individuals). Schools differ enormously in all sorts of ways, depending on such things as whom they cater for, where they are, how they are organized, what their aims are, teaching styles, and so on. However, there is a tendency towards taking for granted that school is more-or-less the same for everyone. Our expectations are also coloured by the way in which schools and teachers are reported and reflected in the media and within different social contexts. Life history allows us to stand back and examine our own and other people's experiences of schooling, as 'data' to be analysed, compared and interpreted, and can lead us to a more considered, better informed view which may reaffirm us in what we are doing or, alternatively, lead to change of some kind (see Weber and Mitchell

1995; Mitchell and Weber 1999). When students embark on courses of initial teacher education they frequently come with a host of preconceptions which can get in the way. For this reason, life history can have an important role in early professional preparation (Troyna and Sikes 1989; Bullough *et al*. 1991; Sikes and Troyna 1991; Bullough 1998).

Life history can help to make theory (of all kinds – sociological, psychological, historical, pedagogical, or whatever) more 'permeable' (Goodson 2001), more accessible and meaningful (see Quicke 1988), and can, thereby, provide a much needed link between theory and practice (Smyth 1982). So, for instance, looking at the educational experiences of students and teachers who are differentially socially, economically, geographically, historically, etc., located, and asking what influence being male, middle-class and heterosexual might have, can cause us to re-examine our practices and adjust our attitudes.

4 *Therapeutic and cathartic benefits in times of crisis.* Teachers are frequently criticized – by parents, employers, politicians, in the media – and blamed for all manner of social ills. Life history work can empirically demonstrate that problems are not the fault of the teachers (Sikes *et al*. 1985; Woods 1985; Woods and Sikes 1987). Such confirmation might alter the balance somewhat in the ongoing game of 'naming and blaming', being played by governments.

In conclusion

We believe that life history work, studies of professional life and work, can enhance our research understandings, broaden and deepen our professional collaboration and develop our professional practices. The value and significance of these transformations can be substantial in terms of furthering our understandings of, as well as developing and improving, teaching and learning.

5 | Life stories and social context: storylines and scripts

Introduction

In general, although people tell their stories in personal, idiosyncratic ways, as we suggested in Chapter 3, they often use storylines derived from the general cultural milieux. In this chapter, we look at the way in which life stories often use 'schematic resources', or 'prior scripts', which not only shape personal narratives but also play a part in shaping the lives of the people who adopt them. As Shotter (1993: 187) says, it depends whether we locate ourselves 'within structures of "already spoken words", or in "words in their speaking" '.

A script to live and work from

The power of prior script is most clearly evident in the work of actors, but sometimes actors, themselves, take over as the authors of 'reality'. Take the movie actor Ronald Reagan who went on to become president of the United States. In reviewing Reagan's capacity to suspend reality, as Shultz puts it, he 'did not believe that what had happened had, in fact, happened'. Reagan, in short, developed a script to live and work from. Shultz says:

> he would go over the 'script' of an event, past or present, in his mind, once that script was mastered, that was the truth – no fact, no argument, no plea for reconsideration, would change his mind.
>
> (Draper 1993: 59)

For Reagan, the script was reality and, given his power, reality was the script. Draper notes: 'in effect, the grade-B pictures' actor was still a grade-B pictures' actor as President. He followed a script, because that was what he had learned to do' (*ibid.*: 59). But then, to some extent, we all tell our own story, albeit in accordance with wider narratives.

Levinson (1979), in his book *Seasons of a Man's Life* (which focuses very narrowly, for not only does he consider only men, but professional men at that), narrates the life story as moving from youth to the articulation of a 'central dream'. Men strive to achieve this dream, which usually involves career promotion and the acquisition of belongings, family and social status, and the point of culmination, collision or collapse is somewhere around forty. This is followed, whether you succeed in your dream or not, by the notion of the mid-life crisis. (In spite of its limitations, Levinson's life cycle model has been adapted and used as a framework for examining the professional life cycle of teachers by Sikes *et al.* (1985) and Huberman (1993).) What follows this mid-life period, in most narratives and most stories that are told, is the beginning of a period of decline and deterioration culminating in death.

In many ways, this narrative of youth, followed by a central professional dream, followed by decline, has represented in a reasonable way the lifespan which was to be expected up until the 1950s or 1960s. With the transformation of medical science and the broadening of life expectancy, these prior scripts, these storylines have become somewhat anachronistic. However, such is the time-lag in redrawing these prior scripts that many life stories are still related in this way thus demonstrating the continuing power of cultural stories to overlay and overlap our more personal modes of storying.

It is only very recently that literature has begun to provide a non-declining story of life for those people between 40 and 60. As Margaret Gullette has argued in a her elegant study of the invention of the mid-life progress novel:

> the difference in the late twentieth century is that the more optimistic minority view of the life course is beginning to appear, in the reiterated and gradually more self-conscious way that lets any new vision become visible. We are seeing the new paradigm – the new ideology – about the middle years shape itself under our reading eyes.
>
> (Gullette 1988: 24)

The new ideology, the new prior script, speaks about a period of progress rather than decline through these years.

Gullette traces the emergence of a new societal storyline in her studies. She says:

> perhaps, to have life-course sequences of a progressive kind in any numbers we had to wait until several favouring circumstances combined in the second half of the twentieth century. Confessional literature became acceptable, while the novel form provided the illusion of privacy for authors who might otherwise have been reticent to appear more confessional even than the poets.
>
> (*ibid.*: 26)

Secondly, she argues:

> a demographic boom provided an audience getting readier, as it aged, to relinquish its original cult of youth; and thus prepared to hear better news about its anxious ageing. Indeed, like a Juggernaut, some part of the mid-life cohort is happy to crush old stereotypes of ageing beneath its future-breasting cart. A postcard, a sweatshirt and a mug keep before us a progressive slogan: 'never trust anyone over ~~30~~, ~~36~~, ~~40~~, 45'. Where economic decline would have placed an intolerable strain on the reading public's willingness to assent to stories of mid-life improvement, the post-war years have been a period of economic boom. Divorce laws and sexual revolution have expanded the choices and attitudes open to adults, and the feminist revolution these open to women.
>
> (*ibid.*: 26)

What Gullette, therefore, is hinting at, is that only now is literature, (and literature is normally ahead of other cultural carriers of ideology), providing us with a different script for the way we story our lives. (See also Hepworth (2000), who suggests that gerontologists can profitably use fictional accounts of ageing to inform their practice.)

What we are searching for here is a way of locating our scrutiny of stories to show that the general forms, schemata, skeletons and ideologies, which we often employ in structuring the way we tell our individual tales, come from the wider culture. Hence, it is an illusion to think that we capture only the person's voice when we capture a personal story. What we capture is a mediation between the personal voice and wider cultural imperatives. In stressing the importance of contextualization, life history makes this mediation explicit (see Chapter 3).

Scholarship scripts

One other instance of a prior script that has become obsolescent as social structures and political possibilities have changed is the script of the 'scholarship boy', which evolved in Britain following the Education Act of 1944 and was most widely performed during the 1950s and 1960s. Of course, scholarships were won by both male and female students, but, given the cultural and gender politics of the peak years for scholarships, it was the part of the boy that was most commonly storied and scripted.

Richard Hoggart (1958), in his influential *The Uses of Literacy*, played an important role in propagating the 'scholarship boy' storyline. In Chapter 10 of the book, entitled 'Unbent springs: a note on the uprooted and anxious', he begins by quoting Tchekov and, later, George Eliot on scholarship boys:

Do, please, write a story of how a young man, the son of a serf, who has been a shop boy, a chorister, pupil of a secondary school, and a university graduate, who has been brought up to respect rank and to kiss the priest's hand, to bow to other people's ideas, to be thankful for each morsel of bread, who has been thrashed many a time, who has had to walk about tutoring without galoshes, who has fought, tormented animals, has been fond of dining at the house of well-to-do relations, and played the hypocrite both to God and man without any need but merely out of consciousness of his own insignificance – describe how that young man squeezes the slave out of himself, drop by drop, and how, awakening one fine morning, he feels running in his veins no longer the blood of a slave but genuine human blood.

(Tchekov, quoted in Hoggart 1958: 241)

For my part I am very sorry for him. It is an uneasy lot at best, to be what we call highly taught and yet not to enjoy: to be present at this great spectacle of life and never to be liberated from a small hungry shivering self.

(Eliot, *ibid*.: 241)

From these quotes, Hoggart begins his exploration of the agony and the ecstasy of the scholarship boy. Writing in 1957, he must be situated in a time and place where in Britain socialist governments had been trying to build a post-war New Jerusalem, based on certain selective versions of social justice and equity. The scholarship boy story, then, stands testimony to a particular version of the progress narrative: one which now stands devalued as reminiscent of outmoded models of meritocracies, masculinities and Marxisms. These factors give Hoggart's text a strongly dated flavour:

It will be convenient to speak first of the nature of the uprooting which some scholarship boys experience. I have in mind those who, for a number of years, perhaps for a very long time, have a sense of no longer really belonging to any group. We all know that many do find a poise in their new situations. There are 'declassed' experts and specialists who go into their own spheres after the long scholarship climb has led them to a PhD. There are brilliant individuals who become fine administrators and officials, and find themselves thoroughly at home. There are some, not necessarily so gifted, who reach a kind of poise which is yet not a passivity nor even a failure in awareness, who are at ease in their new group without any ostentatious adoption of the protective colouring of that group, and who have an easy relationship with their working-class relatives, based not on a form of patronage but on a just respect. Almost every working-class boy who goes through the process of further education by scholarships finds himself chafing against his environment during adolescence. He is at the friction-point of two cultures; the test of his real education lies in his ability, by about the age of twenty-five, to smile at his father with his whole face and to respect his flighty young sister and his slower brother. I shall be concerned with those for whom the uprooting is particularly troublesome, not because I under-estimate the gains which this kind of selection gives, nor because I wish to stress the more depressing features in contemporary life, but because the difficulties of some people illuminate much in the wider discussion of cultural change. Like transplanted stock, they react to a widespread drought earlier than those who have been left in their original soil.

I am sometimes inclined to think that the problem of self-adjustment is, in general, especially difficult for those working-class boys who are only moderately endowed, who have talent sufficient to separate them from the majority of their working-class contemporaries, but not to go much farther. I am not implying a correlation between intelligence and lack of unease; intellectual people have their own troubles: but this kind of anxiety often seems most to afflict those in the working-classes who have been pulled one stage away from their original culture and yet have not the intellectual equipment which would then cause them to move on to join the 'declassed' professionals and experts. In one sense, it is true, no one is ever 'declassed'; and it is interesting to see how this occasionally obtrudes (particularly today, when ex-working-class boys move in all the managing areas of society) – in the touch of insecurity, which often appears as an undue concern to establish 'presence' in an otherwise quite professorial professor, in the intermittent rough homeliness of an important executive and committee-man, in the tendency to vertigo which betrays a lurking sense of uncertainty in a successful journalist.

(Hoggart 1958: 242–3)

The scholarship boy script was employed by a wide range of young men in a variety of different social situations. Ivor (Goodson 1997) has written of his own experience of this storyline, but here it is important to focus on the enormous 'outreach' and influence of this prior script. What follows is a scholarship boy story narrated by a 50-year-old black male teacher who grew up in Belize in Central America:

I suppose that the significant figures that we looked up to were always educated people. Not sports figures or particularly wealthy or people who had made their mark by amassing vast fortunes. When I was growing up, we had a notion of what a good job was: always a job with the civil service. This was British Colonial rule and the civil service was very attractive to us because you got to wear a nice clean white shirt and a tie to go to work, as opposed to coming out from under the bottom of a car all grimy and besmirched but, of course, for a civil service job you

need at least a high school education. But in Belize, where I was growing up, a high school education was not a foregone conclusion. You had
to pay for high school unless you won a government scholarship. It
wasn't a case of applying, everyone who went to elementary school
would take the government scholarship exam in grade six. I'm not sure
exactly what standards they applied, but very few people won those
scholarships. I distinctly recall, because it was a significant item in my
life, that there were thirty-three of us in my grade six class, and I was
the only one who got a scholarship. There was also a church scholarship, but in order to win it you had to be a regular churchgoer. I also
won a church scholarship, together with another pupil, James Robert-
son. Apparently, I had done slightly better than him. I distinctly remember our meeting with some 'authority figures', who explained to me that
this was James's last chance because he was older than I was, and that
I had a very good chance of getting a government scholarship. I don't
know why they didn't just give it to James rather than telling me about
it. As it turned out I did win a government scholarship. When I went to
St. Paul's College, the Anglican high school I attended, which was run
according to the British system, with forms, there were about twenty-
five to thirty of us in the first form. There were about five scholarship
winners, but these had come from all over the country. They were all
Anglicans, of course. The others were paid for by their parents. The
government scholarship was a good thing, because your family just had
to provide the uniform: khaki shorts or long pants, a white shirt with
short sleeves and a green tie. The school sold the tie. We all went around
with green ties, white shirts and khaki pants. When I look back now it
cuts a funny sort of picture, but at that time it was a significant move in
your life. At that time, we felt privileged to go to high school, because
for many of our elementary classmates, that was it – grade six. In Belize,
parents, regardless of a child's academic potential, always felt that a son
should have some sort of trade to fall back on. So, during my elementary years, along with, I suppose, all my contemporaries, I went to learn
a trade. My mother packed my younger brother and myself off to a
tailor. But, in my mind, even though I was very young, I knew very well
that I was not going to be a tailor. I didn't know what I was going to be,
but I was not going to sit in some gloomy tailors' shop and sew clothes
for people all my life, and come out hunch-backed after twenty years of
this, looking for and picking up pieces of thread. I wasn't going to do
that: it would be too stultifying. I suppose way back then I saw myself
as an academic person. As it turned out, this was confirmed by my
experiences. I did very well in elementary school, I suppose it's the same
all over the world, doing well in high school does a whole lot for your
self-esteem and your popularity. People respect you because you
are smart, and that meant all kinds of things. For example, one of the

so-called smart things I displayed was the ability to memorize things. The school always put on plays, and my fantastic memory enabled me to get parts. I was very well respected – Johnson, he's very smart, he's got a future – that type of thing. I remember, earlier than grade four, that I was taken to some classroom where there were some other people, and we had to do a little test. The end result was that I skipped grade five, and went from grade four into grade six. I was very young in grade six. During the first couple of recesses, an old grade four class-mate taunted me with: 'get away from me, you smart Alec!' It's funny how we remember these things while forgetting what happened more recently. My school experiences have always been imprinted on my mind. They were always really encouraging experiences because I was so enthusiastic and so keen. Teachers loved me. When I look back now this was inevitable, I got along with them quite well. In grade four you have a crush on your teacher, and I distinctly recall having a crush on this teacher, Miss Jenkins. She liked me very much. My big thrill was that I would go to her house on Saturdays and wash her bicycle. Bicycles, then, were the way of getting around and, as a result, people took exceedingly good care of them. They would polish them and clean every spoke. After I had washed her bicycle, I could ride it. So there I was, quite proudly tooling around the city, riding Miss Jenkins' bicycle. In a different environment it would be the equivalent of a teacher lending a car. We didn't have bicycles ourselves, so I would visit my class-mates and friends – they knew I was riding Teacher's bicycle. Education officers visited our school, and they appeared to us as powerful figures. They went beyond the white shirt and tie to suit jackets. Very nice. To us, these guys were the pinnacle of professional achievement. We looked up to them.

After that, it was on to St. Paul's College. That was also a very good experience as I continued to be quite enthusiastic and hard working. St. Paul's College had a speech night at the end of every school year. There was a prize for every subject area. Of course, being the academic, highly competitive person I was, I always tried to get a couple of prizes and always did at least win something. I never forget how proud I always made my mother, God rest her soul. It was her son, and this is St. Paul's College. I mean, after all we are talking about a place that had no university. Years after I graduated from high school, there was still no university, which is why I didn't go to university until I left the country. Of course, some people did stick their noses to the grindstone and go to university from there, but I didn't. Speech night was very important because in a class of twenty or thirty boys, two or three would be getting all the prizes. It wasn't that spread out, because it was mainly an Arts School: History, Geography, Language, Health Science, Mathematics – but Algebra and Physical Geometry, no Trigonometry, no

Science. Our school didn't have a science programme at all . . . Later on, when the government opened a technical school in the north part of the city, some of us were encouraged, because they thought we could do it, half way along, to drop a couple of subjects from our regular curriculum. So, for example, I dropped Health Science and Geography and in the evenings I went over to this school and took Chemistry and Physics. But, anyway, that programme didn't work out well because we were well along in our exercises when we had to take the GCE. At that time it was called the Cambridge School Certificate. High school was very enjoyable. A person who has been a prominent person in my life is my High School English teacher, Howard Robinson. He has since gone on to be one of the outstanding intellectuals in the country. He received his BA in English from UCW (University College Wales), and his PhD, with a thesis on the Creole language, as spoken in Belize, in England. He was my mentor throughout my high school years.

After I finished high school I got into teaching. At that time you could enter teaching in two different ways. You could stay on after elementary school and become a teacher's aide, then by taking exams, obtain your first class teacher's certificate. This would take about five years. Alternatively, you could teach once you completed high school. I graduated high school in November and started teaching in January. It makes sense, as far as content is concerned. You certainly learn enough in high school to teach elementary school. In university, PhDs teach MA. There's not that much difference. Once I started teaching, I did in-service training, with courses in methodology, psychology, and class room methods and management. I travelled to the district capital once or twice a week to attend classes. After two years, I received my first class teacher's certificate. About that time a teacher's college opened, but most who went there didn't have high school. I think there was a certain elitist attitude there about high school. I taught elementary for three years from the time I was eighteen . . . I taught elementary for three years in two rural schools. In the second, I was the vice-principal. An older woman was the principal, and I think the powers that be wanted me to stay on and eventually take over the school. But I don't think it was meant to be; I didn't see that as what I really wanted to do. I didn't know what I wanted to do, but I think that way back in my head was always the notion that I would leave Belize, and that I would never want to stay there. It always struck me that it was a place that would eventually end up being quite stifling. That may not be so: I know a lot of my ex-classmates who ended up getting a university education and are quite well placed and they seem to love it. But I think I'm the kind of person who prefers to swim in a larger pond, even though I might be anonymous in that pond, than to rule in a very, very, small little puddle and to move in a sort of almost claustrophobic world. That had never appealed to me. Education is very important in Belize. There is one radio station, Radio Belize. Since there was no university there, anyone leaving the country to study was a news item. The radio would announce: 'departing from Belize Airport today is A, son of B and C of 1 D street, he is making his way to E to study R'. Then four years later, when he returned, the event was announced: 'Conquering Hero'. This was a very important thing, because in a country where high school education couldn't be taken for granted, a person with a degree was a deity – really! You could get a degree in anything and be considered super smart. So, when a person returned to Belize International Airport! Even Cambridge School Certificates were announced on the radio. Students from all over the country got together in Belize City to take the exam in this huge hall, with proctors walking up and down. The exams were then sent to England to be graded and marked. Several months later the results were announced on Radio Belize: they would state the school and the class of the certificate. This radio station was the only one in the whole country, education is a very powerful thing to Belizians; they give education very high value. You want to be one of those announced on the radio for passing your school certificate and, maybe, one day announced as departing the International Airport. I'm just making this connection right now, this powerful thing, imagining the poor guys who didn't make it through high school. You know there is a certain class there, there's a definite thing, you either have a high school education or you don't! You either have a university education or you do not. It's like that. It's funny though, much as they had a university education, obviously something I dreamed of in a way, my not having a university education made it seem too out of reach for me. Because if you wanted to go to university, there were two ways of doing it, you could win a government scholarship or you could have your parents pay for you. Our family couldn't afford it, in fact if I had not won a scholarship to high school I wouldn't have had a high school education.

(Johnson 1993: 1–6)

In the initial narration, George Johnson provides a rich commentary on the power of the scholarship boy script in organizing a life story. As with Reagan, we note how in a real sense the script of a life story narration represents reality in certain ways. If we view the self and identity as ongoing narrative projects, we begin to see the sheer power of the script in organizing and representing reality, both to the self and to others. But, as we noted earlier, the scholarship boy storyline grew out of a social and political milieu of optimistic meritocracy following the Second World War. Resources were limited but growing, and for a minority of the working class there was the potential for social mobility. This potential, this window of opportunity, was celebrated in the scholarship boy story. The scholarship boy represented a particular selectivity of class, gender and race at a particular historical moment.

In the event, this moment passed and in the hiatus of the 1960s was effectively deconstructed. But for those who had scripted their lives on this storyline, the story continued as their chosen representation of reality. One of the fascinations of collaborating on life story narrations is to see how intensive grounded conversations and introspective reflection combine to allow the life story tellers to 'locate' their stories. George Johnson spoke of this process towards the end of collaborating on his life story when historical and sociological insights began to provide the material for him to locate his story:

> Looking back, I feel I betrayed the academic promise I showed as a child. Examining the tapes and transcripts had dislodged a number of memories and subsequent feelings. On Monday, I felt quite depressed; I realize that life had passed by. I was troubled by thoughts of what should have been. At this age I should be a professor or an executive with a house and car. Where have twenty-five years gone?
>
> A university degree is very important to me; I always envied those who returned to Belize with one. I appreciate there are complex reasons behind this. Part of me doubts my ability to do university studies. I don't know if I've got what it takes. However, at some stage, I made choices. I avoided putting my abilities to the test. Although I didn't articulate it at the time, now, on reflection, I escaped. I chose a different path. I was a womanizer who ignored my intellectual potential. Eventually, I chose marriage over studies. Within my own family, my stepfather, a driver, was an incorrigible womanizer. In high school, despite my academic success, I was rebellious and made trouble for the teacher, largely through my quick wit. I avoided further education, but felt frustrated. I know I perceived leaving St. Paul's for Honduras as running away, because I didn't want to be trapped. I knew I wanted a university degree but wasn't prepared to face the challenge, so I quit. I didn't want to be edged out; I didn't want to be an anachronism.
>
> Honduras seemed the logical choice since I was born there. I now see this journey as a flight from self, or from destiny. Only by attending university could I be announced: 'arriving at the airport . . .'. I don't really know whether I wanted that, living out a culturally provided script.
>
> (*ibid.*: 73–4)

The examples of mid-life progress narratives and scholarship boy stories show the potentially intimate relationship between social and political circumstances and cultural storylines. In a real sense, social structures may push storylines in particular directions and the stories then legitimate the structures, and so on, in a self-legitimating circle. The relationship between social structure and story is loosely coupled, and stories can resist as well as enhance the imperatives of structure. But, in either case, the story stands in relationship to social structure. The scholarship boy story is a particular example of this: a 'celebration' of a particular historical moment of opportunity for a selective group of male students, sometimes of working-class origin.

The storyline then, privileges some; more significantly, however, it silences the many: as a storyline, it silences women; it silences most of the non-scholarship working class, and it silences whole nations and racial groups where such windows of opportunity do not exist. With the passing of the scholarship boy, we see the long overdue end of a storyline; but, as we have seen, when life storylines become obsolescent in the wider cultural setting, this leaves a good deal of rehabilitation and reformation to be undertaken at the level of the narrative project of the self.

In studying scholarship girls, a good deal of work has been undertaken, most notably in Germany. Interestingly, Erika Hoerning (1985) has explored the relevance of social mobility and scholarship success to women's stories. Her work follows Hoggart in exploring the tension between storylines that work in the family of origin, and those that work in the wider professional milieux. Contact with the family of origin was kept through a 'same old girl' storyline, whilst a new institutional milieu led to the construction of identity as a 'new professional woman'. Hoerning concludes:

> The women studied in this project attempt to remain in contact with their original milieu by proving themselves with tried and true virtues (such as helping with the housework, the readiness to comply, and promoting less controversial discussions when at home). In doing so, they assume that their parents, brothers, sisters, and so on are capable of modifying their normative conceptions of female careers, but do not realize that by adopting these means of getting along they are seen as prototypes of their original milieu in the eyes of their family, and as such do not represent their new milieu at all. The desired effect – the parents' acknowledgment of their daughter's current life course – is probably not produced for various reasons. First, the family of origin simply does not know how to support its daughter in her current stage of life; secondly, the family most likely thinks that they are losing their ability to influence strongly a daughter who is drifting away from them. They do not understand the rules and norms of their daughter's new milieu, nor do they feel that they have the right to judge them. If these female social ascenders accept the consequences of this situation, they diminish contact with their old milieu or perhaps even cut it off completely. Formulas for co-existence must be developed for the amount of contact which does remain, formulas which act to screen the women's new, estranged identities. When the afore-mentioned tried and true virtues of the old

milieu (helping with the housework, readiness to comply, etc.) are reactivated during the few visits which still take place, then these actions can be seen as co-existence formulas in practice. Parents are not required to love their daughter and accept her new course of life because this new course has proved to be satisfying to her; rather, they do these things because – in spite of their daughter's new course of life – she is still the 'same old girl'.

(Hoerning 1985: 109–10)

In conclusion

The collection of stories then, especially the mainstream stories that live out a prior script, will merely fortify patterns of domination. We shall need to move from life stories to life histories, from narratives to genealogies of context, towards a modality that embraces 'stories of action within theories of context'. In so doing, stories might be seen as the social constructions they are, providing glimpses in their location within power structures and social milieux. Stories then, provide a starting point for active collaboration, 'a process of deconstructing the discursive practices through which one's subjectivity has been constituted' (Middleton 1992: 20). Only if we deal with stories as the starting point for collaboration, as the beginning of a process of coming to know, will we come to understand their meaning, to see them as social constructions which allow us to locate and interrogate the social world in which they are embedded.

Shotter has spoken of the need to focus on the process of becoming somebody. He asks:

if life has become an improvisatory art, and adjusting to discontinuity is not an idiosyncratic problem of one's own, but the emerging problem of our time, what is involved in becoming the authors of our own lives?

(Shotter 1993: 189)

Here, Shotter is arguing that the condition of postmodernity is changing the modalities of authorship of storylines and social schemata. He follows many of the same lines of enquiry that Kenneth Gergen follows in his book, *The Saturated Self*. Gergen writes of the new technologies of communication we are immersed in:

It is my central thesis that this immersion is propelling us toward a new self-consciousness: the postmodern. The emerging commonplaces of communication . . . are critical to understanding the passing of both the romantic and modern views of self. What I call the *technologies of social saturation* are central to the contemporary erasure of individual self . . . There is a *populating of the self*, reflecting the infusion of partial identities through social saturation. And there is the onset of a *multiphrenic* condition, in which one begins to experience the vertigo of unlimited multiplicity. Both the populating of the self and the multi-phrenic condition are significant preludes to postmodern conscious-ness.

(Gergen 1991: 49)

Gergen here sets the postmodern possibilities for storying against romantic and modernist schemata. In the latter cases, the Enlightenment Project was predominant in the development of storyline. Sequential and unitary stories were developed which presented a world that could be rationally ordered and recounted. Such a rationally conceived world can be set against what Shotter (1993) calls 'the imaginary' – a world of emergence, of process, of becoming, of multiplicity and unpredictability:

It is still too easy for us to think that when we argue about such things as 'society', the 'individual', 'the person', 'identity', 'the citizen', 'civil society', 'thought', 'speech', 'language', 'desire', 'perception', 'moti-vation', etc., and plan a research project upon any one of them, we all know perfectly well what 'it' is that is represented by the concepts we use in our arguments, and what 'it' is that we are researching into. We find it difficult to accept that 'objects' such as these are not already 'out there' in the world in some primordial naturalistic sense. The idea that they are 'essentially contested' concepts; that they only 'make sense' as they are developed within a discourse; that such entities either have an imaginary component to them or are wholly or radically imaginary; that they are 'entities' (hidden) within the movement of process, which do not at first have a distinctive existence as such at all, but which, in the continued 'movement' of the process, emerge as an identifiable part of it, all that is radically alien to us.

(Shotter 1993: 198–9)

This means that, in scrutinizing life stories, we need increasingly to make space for the emergent story, as well as the prenarrated Enlightenment Script. Moving from the singularly narrated life story to the collaboratively generated life history is one strategy to create such spaces (although if con-ducted in certain ways, it can be a new modality of ordering and sequence) The life history should focus on emergent categories, on process, on move-ment, as well as on stability and static notion of context.

As well as the data's being distinctive, so too then are the aspirations of life story and life history. In the first case, the intention is to understand the person's view and account of their life, the story they tell about their life. As W. Thomas famously said: 'if men define situations as real, they are real in their consequences'. In the life history, the intention is to understand the pat-terns of social relations, interactions and constructions in which the lives of women and men are embedded. The life history pushes the question whether private issues are also public matters; the life story individualizes and personalizes; the life history contextualizes and politicizes.

In moving from life stories towards life histories, we move from singular narration to include other documentary sources and oral testimonies. It is important to view the self as an emergent and changing 'project', not a stable and fixed entity. Over time, our view of ourselves changes and so, therefore, do the stories we tell about ourselves. In this sense, it is useful to view self-definition as an ongoing narrative project.

6 | Questions of ethics and power in life history research

Introduction

Research per se is an inherently political activity in that it has a bearing on how human beings make sense of their world. Consequently, because it impacts upon people, all research potentially involves ethical issues and considerations. The implications of this, for anyone touched, in any way, by any particular research project, vary tremendously, from the insignificant to the life altering. Furthermore, the sphere of influence of research can range from the idiosyncratic and local to the global. Everyone alive has been affected in some way, however tangentially, by research projects with which they have had no personal involvement. Consider, for example, spin-offs from space programme research or, maybe less obviously, work on genetically modified foods or in the field of gender studies. With regard to this last, 'findings' and altering theoretical explanations and understandings about 'differences' between men and women's experiences, perceptions and motivations (for instance) can have repercussions far beyond the local circumstances in which they were formulated. This is because, informed by particular understandings generated by the research, people will view women and men in very different local circumstances in this light. These perceptions may come to have concrete, and therefore ethical, consequences for people's lives if policy and practice are affected by them.

If people who are distant from research can be affected by it, how much more so those who are intimately involved. In this chapter, our aim is to focus on ethical issues associated with, and which can arise in, the conduct of life history research. Our main concern is with the implications for informants, and we concentrate on three areas (without, of course, wishing to suggest that these are the only areas where ethical issues occur):

1 Research design and conduct.
2 The nature of the topics that life historians tend to study, allied with the nature of the methodology.

3 Claims that life history research can be emancipatory and empowering.

Before moving on to consider each of these separately, we need to be clear about what we mean by ethics and ethical issues and concerns. Thus, in the context of research, ethical issues and concerns are generally understood to be associated with the following:

1 with what constitutes a 'legitimate' focus/topic of research;
2 with the conduct of (all stages and aspects of) the research;
3 with the behaviour of researchers;
4 with standards and/or codes of practice; in short, with 'acceptable' ways of doing things;
5 with broad issues of 'voice', values and validity.

The key ethical consideration is how the research affects the people whose experiences, perceptions, behaviours, attitudes, or whatever, are the focus of the study and who are the designated 'research population'. In the case of life history, we are talking specifically about 'informants'. Compared with populations for other types of research, life history informants are required to make a considerable commitment in terms of time and intimacy of involvement. Depending on the specific study, the exact amount of involvement will vary, but even in those cases where there is only one, relatively brief, interview session, the informant does have actively and (we would suggest) consciously, to be a collaborating participant. This means that questions to do with whether it is ethical for research to be conducted covertly, without the knowledge of the research population, are unlikely to arise, or more precisely, are unlikely to arise in the same way as they might in, for instance, observational ethnographic studies. On the other hand, the level of intimacy involved in life history research does in itself increase the potential for harm and, therefore, poses a different batch of ethical questions. For this reason, blanket ethical research codes do have their limitations. Our recommendation is that each instance is considered in its own light.

Having said this, it seems self-evident that the fundamental ethical requirement laid on all life history researchers is that informants' rights as people, as individuals, as selves, as subjects, as autonomous beings, should, at all times, be respected. It is hard to imagine anyone questioning this, given that (Kantian) respect for persons lies at the root of liberal democratic society, and is the basis of generally accepted moral thinking on right and wrong (i.e. moral) ways of behaving towards others. However, as Robson (1993: 30) points out, using an example of an experiment which involves sewing up kittens' eyelids, it is possible for a researcher to act in accordance with an ethical code of practice but still be deemed to have behaved immorally (even if it is animals rather than people who are the 'victims'). The point is that the issues and dilemmas are complex and situationally specific. A further complication is that, particularly perhaps in the case of life history research, it is not always possible to predict the sort of harm that informants may experience as a consequence of their involvement. This is not an opt-out for life historians but rather an injunction laid on them to give proper thought and attention to what they are doing and to the potential difficulties which can arise.

Research design and conduct

The fundamental reason why researchers choose to use a life history approach is because they believe that detailed, personal information about how people have perceived and experienced things that have happened in their lives will enable them to better understand whatever it is they are studying. Thus, Pat wanted to know about the ways in which teachers' experiences of being parents might have had implications for how they approached their work. Having children is a universal experience but, at the same time, it is distinctly personal and intimate involving, as it does, relationships, sex, emotional commitments, medical histories, values and beliefs, desires and disappointments, financial considerations, and so on. Such a study, in common with, for example, Andrew Sparkes's (1995) life history work with lesbian and gay physical education teachers, and Audrey Osler's (1997) with black teachers, is clearly likely to touch on deeply personal, private and possibly painful matters, and researchers and informants will be aware of this from the start. However, life history studies looking at career choice, subject affinity, professional socialization and development, discipline maintenance and teaching styles might equally end up in difficult territory (see, for example, Ball and Goodson 1985; Sikes *et al.* 1985; Bullough *et al.* 1991) Researchers need to be aware of such possibilities and of the implications for informants when they decide to take a life history approach.

Researchers also need to guard against letting sheer nosiness and any voyeuristic or prurient tendencies get the better of them, leading them into questions and areas which may not be justifiable given the declared focus of the study This may sound extreme, but it is the case that life historians do tend to be nosy and curious and that, given the rare luxury of talking about oneself, informants may be seduced into revealing more about themselves than they would normally consider judicious. Simply satisfying personal curiosity is, perhaps, unethical when it is cloaked in a research context. And then, there is the further question of what happens to the information gleaned. Knowledge is power and knowing something about someone puts the researcher into a potentially powerful situation. Again, this may sound extreme and alarmist, and in most cases there are unlikely to be any problems. However, in the context of her work as a PGCE tutor, Pat did once have the experience of coming across a headteacher who, as a head of department a decade before in another local education authority, had been an informant to a life history project. Things that he had told her then, about his professional beliefs and his private life, were distinctly at odds with his present self and position and caused both him and Pat some embarrassment, and even led Pat to wonder whether her institution should continue to use his school for student placements. This example raises yet more ethical questions about personal and professional responsibility and about the ways in which different roles can overlap – but this is the reality of research, a reality which is rarely admitted in most research texts.

An associated consideration involves whom informants are to be. In Chapter 2, we referred to the potential problems of doing life history work 'in one's own backyard' with colleagues, friends, relatives and acquaintances. Delving into personal details with people that you know, can cause ethical dilemmas which are no less significant or real for being unanticipated. You never know what you are going to find out and how it might affect perceptions, relationships, and even someone's tenure of a particular job. It may be an extreme and unlikely example, but what would a researcher do if, in the course of a life history interview, someone revealed that they had paedophiliac yearnings (see Sikes 2000a)? Where would the ethical responsibility lie then? To the informant, or to children? It may be easy enough to make a decision in a hypothetical situation, but in reality the situation may not seem quite so clear-cut. Furthermore, assurances of confidentiality and anonymity, basic tenets of most ethical codes, are by no means simple and straightforward when it comes to life history work because of the personal and idiosyncratic information that is involved and which ultimately will probably be recorded, reported and re-presented in some way. It may be extremely difficult, if not impossible, to guarantee total anonymity without substantially altering accounts, and whereas in some circumstances this may be justifiable, in others it may require changes of such an order that the work can no longer be considered as life history. Again, this may not matter, but it may have implications for research design in the first instance. For example, a fictionalized approach may turn out to be the best way of utilizing rich life history data, capitalizing on the benefits of the methodology whilst protecting the privacy of informants.

A major consideration in discussions of research ethics concerns the extent to which researchers should be open and honest about what it is that they are studying and how they are studying it. In some cases researchers have justified covert studies on the basis that they would never have got access, or information or 'truth' had they been totally up-front about their work. Studies of powerful groups or individuals, or investigations into socially unacceptable or even illegal attitudes, behaviours and practices are examples of research which it may be difficult or impossible to conduct without some degree of deception. As we have noted, life history requires the active participation of informants. It is in essence to some degree collaborative, however explicitly articulated this characteristic may be. Some commentators have suggested that such collaboration can act as an ethical safeguard (see, for example, Lincoln and Guba 1989) ensuring 'proper' treatment of informants. Even so, it is possible for life historians to be economical with the truth without their being outright liars, raising question marks over the degree to which informants can be considered to have given their 'informed consent' to involvement. The scope for deception is, inevitably, wide, and is there in all phases of the research process. For example, Measor and Sikes (1992: 217–21) describe how, in inviting teachers to take part in a life history study, they were a little cagey. Thus they failed to mention how much time might be involved, thinking this might put some people off. Given that their research was taking a grounded theory approach, they were genuinely unable to be specific about the focus of the work, but what informants thought about the veracity of this is perhaps another issue. Maybe, compared for instance to failing to tell potential informants that one is investigating racist attitudes, Measor and Sikes's economies with the truth were minor. Nevertheless, the fact remains that they were not totally open. In designing and planning research it is important to consider what position is going to be taken with regard to openness, and to formulate a justification in cases where total honesty is not employed.

It would, of course, be perfectly possible to do life history research in a totally covert manner, under the guise of friendship. In other words, the researcher and the 'friend' would have seemingly 'natural' conversations, which the researcher would record in some way, either through notes or even by means of a concealed tape recorder. These recorded conversations could then be taken away and treated as data to be worked upon and eventually re-presented. Whether or not such a deception was planned, or even if the opportunity presented itself in the course of a developing relationship, it would surely be hard to justify it as ethical research practice. The 'informant' would have been used and their friendship abused. This would be a clear example of what Patti Lather (1986: 263) has termed 'rape research', that is, research where the researcher takes what they want and then departs without any concern for or further contact with their informant. Less obvious, but also potentially ethically dubious, are those occasions where researchers deliberately manipulate relationships with informants, frequently by employing techniques of 'reciprocity', with a view to obtaining better quality data.

Reciprocity was initially suggested as a counterpoint to the 'scientific' notion and practice of interviewing as an information-gathering tool. In a much quoted article, Oakley (1981) argued that paradigms of traditional interviewing practice were masculine paradigms and inimical to feminist research. Whilst this was an important observation, and one which did have the effect of interrupting taken-for-granted notions of interviewing, it is not without its own problems both with regard to its value and status as a 'feminist research strategy', and in the degree to which it actually can be 'non-hierarchical' and 'non-exploitative'. As Pat has suggested:

> 'Reciprocity' (Oakley, 1981), which occurs when the female interviewer shares personal information with the female informant, is regarded as good feminist practice (Cosslett, 1994; Nielsen, 1990; Stanley, 1990), because it is believed to result in interviews which are less exploitative and hierarchical than those where the interviewer just asks the questions. Sharing information in order to be, or to appear to be, less exploitative can be seen to be instrumental and manipulative rather than socially supportive, and nor does it get away from the fundamental question of who is sharing with whom. As Ann Phoenix writes:
>
> > while it is sometimes very comfortable to be a feminist researcher interviewing women, that cosiness does not simply come from shared gender but is often partly the result of shared social class and/or shared colour. The interview relationship is partly dependent on the relative positions of investigators and informants in the social formation. Simply being women discussing 'women's issues' in the context of a research interview is not sufficient for the establishment of rapport and the seamless flow of an interview. (1994, p. 50)
>
> And, once again, adherence to a 'pure' notion of reciprocity limits the scope of feminist research because it pre-empts the possibility of interviewing men. Finally, and in my view most importantly, it is essential to remember that when it comes to interviewing, the key factor which usually determines how successful the encounter will be both in terms of the data it yields and as a social interaction, is how the two people get on. Reciprocity with someone you don't like is impossible, regardless of their sex.
>
> (Sikes 1997: 21)

Furthermore, reciprocity simply in order to get good data can be seen as, and can be, ethically questionable even though it can at the same time be presented as yet another means of involving and collaborating with informants. Bertaux (1981: 20), for example, has claimed that reciprocity leads to data which 'becomes mutually shared knowledge, rooted in the intersubjectivity of the interaction'. He goes on to quote Catani who suggests that, 'the price to be paid by the observer will be to be reciprocally known just as thoroughly by the object' (*ibid.*); although there is, of course, always a possibility that the informant has no interest in knowing about the researcher (see Munro 1998: 127).

And yet, as we have discussed earlier, informants have expectations about research situations and this colours the researcher/informant relationship. Provided the research is not covert, such relationships are known, by both parties, to be of a specific type and for a particular purpose. This is not to say that friendships cannot develop, but such friendships are separate and not usual, not least because frequently, as Martyn Hammersley indicates:

What is involved in the process of self-disclosure [when used as a research strategy] is the presentation of those aspects of one's self and life that provide a bridge for building relationships with participants, and the suppression of those which constitute a possible barrier.

(quoted in Measor and Sikes 1992: 215)

Staying with the question of how informants regard the research enterprise, it is worth referring back to a consideration that was raised in Chapter 2: namely, the way in which life history interviews can resemble Rogerian counselling sessions. There are a number of issues here. Firstly, it is incumbent upon the researcher to make it clear that they are researchers and not counsellors. Their primary aim is to do research and to collect data. Even where this has been done, informants may still take on a client as opposed to informant type of role. When this happens there are ethical implications. What does the researcher, what does anyone do, if a fellow human asks for guidance or advice? If participating in a research project has been the catalyst for self-doubt or personal questioning of some kind, then maybe, because they are responsible for bringing the informant to this pass, there is some ethical responsibility upon the researcher to help them deal with the situation. With the best will in the world, and with all the explanation and openness there could possibly be, the potential for reflection leading to a personal crisis is there. Of course, such things can happen in other types of research and in other areas of life; however, the fact remains that there is a greater likelihood of its happening in life history work because of the nature of the methodology and as a result of the aspects of life it tends to explore. Consequently, researchers need to have thought about what they will do if such a situation does arise.

Ethical issues arise when it comes to writing up. Questions around whose story is being told, as discussed in Chapter 3, inevitably have ethical aspects. Earlier on, we referred to problems concerning confidentiality and anonymity as being particularly pertinent for life historians. How to deal with these problems demands careful thought right from the initial planning and design stage.

Staying with dilemmas around writing up: in telling a story there is a temptation to make the narrative as exciting and as engaging as possible. Linda Wagner-Martin (1998) has suggested that this tendency leads to certain groups', and especially to women's, becoming invisible because their lives may seem too 'boring' and 'ordinary' to be worth recording or studying. Another consequence of what might be described as the 'dramatic imperative', can be a sort of othering, an 'essentializing', an exoticization of individuals in order to make the point more forcefully. Such othering can have negative repercussions, regardless of the imperializing tendencies it can reflect. Once again, researchers need to be on their guard. Traditionally, and in the early days of the Chicago school especially, the life histories which were produced were, almost without exception, of 'marginal' or 'deviant' folk, of people who in obvious ways were out of the ordinary – Native American chiefs, transsexuals, tramps, crooks. Yet, one thing that life history research makes plain is that everyone is 'unusual', out of the ordinary in some way or other, that everyone has a story to tell. The ethical danger lies in overdoing the differences, making informants into some sort of freak show, and thereby denying them basic human respect by inviting others to gaze upon them. The line separating sensationalizing, voyeurism and prurience is a narrow one.

The nature of the topics that life historians tend to study allied with the nature of the methodology

Given that life history research is primarily concerned with the ways in which all and any life events potentially influence and impact upon all experiences, perceptions, beliefs, values and so on, it inevitably deals with personal and, therefore, sensitive topics: topics which can carry a heavy ethical responsibility for researchers who broach or focus on them in their work.

Lee and Renzetti define a sensitive topic as:

> one that potentially poses for those involved a substantial threat, the emergence of which renders problematic for the researcher and/or the researched, the collection, holding and/or dissemination of research data.
>
> (Lee and Renzetti 1993: 5)

They go on to suggest that the following can be identified as areas of (at least, potential) sensitivity in research:

1 where research intrudes into the private sphere or some deeply personal experience;
2 where a 'deviance' is the focus of study;
3 where research impinges on the interests of those in positions of power;
4 where researchers are investigating religious practices, articles or beliefs subject to profanation.

All of these can be relevant to life historians researching aspects of teachers' lives and careers, but it is perhaps the first, where research intrudes into the private sphere of some deeply personal experience, that will most frequently cause ethical dilemmas for them.

As we have said on a number of occasions, it is not always possible to know when a topic or issue will turn out to be sensitive. Lee and Renzetti talk about different cultural groups having different sensitivities and how a topic that a researcher approaches with caution can turn out to be innocuous, and vice versa (1993: 5). Cultural groups are one thing; individual lives are yet another, because we can never know personal sources of stress or pain or what effect talking about them may have. Pat learnt this lesson quite forcefully when she was a young researcher working on the life history study reported in Sikes *et al.* (1985). The key focus of this work was to investigate, 'how individuals adapted to, or sought to change, situations; how they managed roles and constraints; and . . . their perceptions of their careers' (p. 11). Secondary school art and science teachers of different ages and career stages were simply invited to tell their life stories with particular reference to their work. There was no interview schedule and interviewers took a prompting, interrogative role rather than a directive one. Thus, they let the informant carry the tale wherever they wanted to, although they would seek clarification and elaboration on occasion. The interview-conversations which ensued from this approach were detailed, wide-ranging, stretched, in most cases, over many hours, and resulted in vast amounts of data. Two informants, in particular, led Pat to have concerns associated with the ethics of what she was involved in. In the first case, the topic was actually perhaps more sensitive, more threatening for Pat than it was for Dave, the informant.

At the time of the research, Dave was a 44-year-old senior teacher and the head of science at his school. He was keen and eager to be involved in the study when approached, and was something of a 'key informant'. He talked at length about how he had gone into teaching despite being expected to become a partner in his father's prosperous business. He described his changing relationships with students as he got older, his attitude to discipline, his subject, pedagogy, the part that school played in his life, his shifting career aspirations and achievements, and about the way in which *all* of his personal and professional beliefs and values changed when his 9-year-old son developed leukaemia, had a long and distressing illness, and had subsequently died five years previously. Dave clearly found it painful to talk about his son but was equally clearly determined to do so:

James' death was the most significant thing that's ever happened to me. I hope it's the worst thing that will ever happen to me. It's hard to imagine anything that could touch it and everything was changed by it. You expect your parents to die, it's possible that your wife will, but your kids shouldn't. It's obscene. It turns the order of everything arse about face and you can't see things in the same way. Whilst James was ill I kept thinking he'd get better. I couldn't believe that he could die. I watched him suffering and I wanted it to be me. I'd come into school, and it was bloody hard sometimes, there were all these children, healthy children, evil bastards some of them and there was my boy, dying. It's a bit of a contradiction but I did bury myself in work. I worked, worked,

worked to escape from what was going on at home. It wasn't fair on my wife – and she'd resigned to spend time with him. But I ran away a bit. If I'm going to talk about influences on my career then I've **GOT** to talk about James. It's all right. It hurts, yes, but not talking about him, ignoring him, would be worse.

(Sikes *et al.* 1985)

At that time, Pat had no personal experience of death, nor any children of her own. She found Dave's story threatening because of her own fears about the death of a loved one and because of the pain she imagined it would be causing him. Despite Dave's assurances to the contrary, she felt that this was an unacceptably sensitive topic to be discussing in research, albeit life history research, about teaching as a career. However, as Dygregrov and Dygregrov (1999: 655) point out: 'some respondents talk about their experiences (of the death of their children) all the time; therefore, talking about them in an interview situation will not be particularly distressing – rather normal', and even helpful and comforting. Now, many years and many deaths down the line, Pat knows that this is, indeed, the case – for some people, but by no means all. Maybe one answer to ethical difficulties arising out of sensitive topics is simply to leave to the informant the decision about whether to talk about a particular issue: obviously, it is wholly unethical to pursue a topic when an informant does not wish to talk about it. Conversely, it is worth pointing out that there may be times when it is the researcher who is 'at risk' of harm because a topic is sensitive to them. Again, owing to the nature of life history research, it is not always possible to predict what topics will arise and when. It is important, though, to be aware of the possibility.

The other experience which worried Pat concerned Keith, a 38-year-old chemistry teacher, who had joined the profession only two years before, having been made redundant from his previous job. Keith had five children. He had become a teacher because he had fond recollections of his own grammar school days. The reality he found confronting him in the comprehensive where he worked was very different from what he had expected. Not to put too fine a point on it, he hated teaching. Over the conversation-interview sessions he talked about what he disliked, how miserable he felt, and how his relationships at home were being affected by his unhappiness. On the fifth or so interview he greeted Pat by telling her that he had resigned and that it was thanks to her and her invitation to talk about his career. Pat was appalled. She felt responsible that this man with major financial commitments was out of work. Visions of hungry children and a wife working all the hours God sent crowded in. If Keith had not taken part in the life history project none of this would have happened. Or would it? On one level, assuming responsibility for someone else's decision can be seen as reflecting an inflated sense of importance and agency. Talking to Keith afterwards, when he was settled in a well-paid job as a pharmaceutical representative,

Pat came to the view that the research had been a catalyst for his radical action but that it would have happened eventually, regardless. The opportunity to reflect on how he was experiencing teaching and to articulate his misery had brought forward his leaving and, in the long run, had had a positive outcome. Nevertheless, the ethical question does remain. Maybe the examples presented here are not in the same unethical league as, say, Laud Humphries' (1970) covert investigation of gays, Milgram's (1963) study of obedience involving fake electric shocks, or Jane Elliott's (see Peters 1987) experiment, in which a class of children were put into a situation where they both experienced and practised discrimination and prejudice. Nevertheless, we cannot emphasize strongly enough that participating in life history research can damage the psychological and emotional (not to mention, as in Keith's case, financial) health of informants, and of researchers too. It is not to be embarked upon lightly.

Claims that life history research can be emancipatory and empowering

Life history methodology has the potential to enable 'ordinary' individuals to tell their story, to give their version, to 'name their silent lives' (to adopt McLaughlin and Tierney's (1993) much quoted title). This potential has made the approach very popular with feminists and, more generally, with researchers working for social justice who wish to demonstrate and then question sexual, racial, gender, social class, ability, religious (and so on) differentiation and bias in a way that other research methods cannot (see Giroux 1991). Along with certain other qualitative methods, it has been frequently claimed that life history research can be a socially empowering and emancipatory experience for informants, an experience that can change their lives for the better. It is our view, however, that claims for empowerment and emancipation through research in general, and life history in particular, are, at best, naïve and, at worst, grandiose and ethically dubious (see Troyna 1994; Sikes *et al.* 1996). Research approaches which make such claims might even:

> have weaknesses which may prove incapacitating. If this is so we may be advocating genres of inquiry in the name of empowerment, whilst at the same time effectively disempowering the very causes and people we seek to serve.
>
> (Goodson 1995: 89)

In this section, we want to look at ethical issues around life history research as emancipatory and empowering because there has been a tendency to be celebratory rather than critical and there is a case for caution of which researchers should be aware.

Empowerment and emancipation are generally considered to ensue from a number of different yet interrelated sources. The chief of these are discussed in the following sections.

Appeals to 'better nature': the power of subjective experience

Empowerment will come about after the changes to social policy and practice, which will result when those in power are able to hear how life really is for women, gays, minority ethnic group members, schoolteachers, the differently abled, the poor, and so on. In other words, people whose stories are not normally told because their lives are not considered sufficiently important or significant (Wagner-Martin 1998: 92). The theory is that policy-makers and those with hegemonic power do not know what life is like for those who are differently positioned, socially, from them. When they find out they will be morally impelled to make changes. For example, when Reagan was president of the United States, a story (we do not know whether or not it was apocryphal) went round about a young woman he met on the campaign trail who explained, in some detail, why she would be unable to go to college because of the financial cost. Apparently, the president was appalled and asked how such a state of affairs could arise. What he had failed to realize was that the policies and legislation his government had introduced had implications and consequences for real-life individuals. Whilst the young woman concerned was said to have been given personal help, others in similar positions were not. On one level, her telling her story was emancipatory for her, but she was the only person to benefit.

A major drawback with this line of argument lies in getting those in a position to do something about a situation, to read (or otherwise learn about) life history. It is one thing to note that one of the strengths of life history is its accessibility in terms of its being relatively jargon-free and easy and interesting to read compared with other types of research writing; it is quite another to guarantee that it will be read by a non-academic audience. And yet, researchers do sometimes imply, or suggest more strongly, that their work may lead to change through 'giving voice'. If this suggestion is used to persuade people to participate in research, we would suggest that the researcher is either ingenuous or using unethical strategies, in that informants are being involved under false pretences.

It is also impossible to predict how stories of discrimination or disadvantage will be heard and interpreted. Plenty of people, including those in positions of power, hold values and beliefs in which what might be termed negative differentiation is fundamental. They are unlikely to be moved in any way by life histories and there will not, therefore, be any emancipatory or empowering effects.

Empowerment through enhanced self-worth

The rallying cry of the women's liberation movement of the 1960s and 1970s was that 'the personal is political'. The message was that the life stories of 'ordinary women' should be contextualized and turned into life histories in order to demonstrate the ways in which external forces of all kinds can shape and determine life courses and experiences. People's lives cannot be lived independently of how they are socially positioned: in other words, it can be extremely difficult to do things which are not, socially, deemed to be appropriate for someone who possesses, or is attributed with, particular characteristics. Rather than blaming oneself for failure to achieve or for depression stemming from frustration and a sense of being constrained, life histories can reveal that personal, individual experiences and perceptions actually have their origins in social forces. This can have an emancipatory and empowering effect in that it removes or alleviates the personal sense of responsibility and gives pointers as to where change might be possible. Denzin (1970) recognizes this in remarking that, 'life history may be the best method for studying adult socialization, the situational response of self to daily interactional contingencies'. Many life history studies have picked up on this potential and claimed it as a justification for using the approach (see, for example, Sikes *et al.* 1985; Casey 1993; Thiessen *et al.* 1996; Munro 1998).

On a slightly different level, knowing that someone is sufficiently interested in your life to hear your story and work it into a life history can be empowering in that it can enhance one's sense of self-worth. Feeling positive about oneself and knowing that you are valued is, perhaps, one of the most empowering states of being, regardless of any concrete changes which may ensue (see Clandinin and Connelly 1998: 249). However, for this value to be realized, it is important that informants should not feel that they have been badly used and that their story is being used simply to meet the researcher's needs.

Empowerment through sharing stories: you are not alone

Ken Plummer (1995) has written about the way in which reading the life stories and histories of others who have similar characteristics, backgrounds, experiences and perceptions, can be empowering and emancipatory because it can show an individual that they are not alone. Learning how someone else has dealt with the situations that we face can be extremely empowering because it provides a model, a way to proceed, which we can adopt, adapt or reject. Indeed, making teachers' stories available for others to consider was a major aim of Sikes *et al.*s' (1985) teachers' careers project:

> knowledge of how others have come to terms with the system, coped with the problems and made their individual contributions might

increase the prospects for personal satisfaction, and the redefinition of situations more in line with personal aspirations.

(Sikes *et al*. 1985: 12)

Of course, there is always the possibility that people will not be able to recognize or identify with the life histories that are presented. Where this happens, the experience could be diminishing and undermining, rather than empowering. Life historians must guard against setting up icons or stereotypes and against failing to make explicit multiple differences and possibilities.

Empowerment through participation in non-hierarchical research

We have repeatedly referred to the way in which life history research is in essence a collaborative methodology. The life historian cannot proceed unless informants agree to tell their stories and then they have to assume and trust that the story they are told is 'true', in so far as there is no deliberate intention to lie and deceive (see Sikes 2000a). The degree and nature of collaboration as it is built into the design of any research project varies, depending on aims and objectives. Goodson, for example, has been keen to advocate a high level of collaboration (see Goodson and Fliesser 1994, 1995; Goodson and Mangan 1995; Sikes *et al*. 1996). When life history research has a distinctly developmental function, when a key aim is professional and personal development, then collaboration and co-working will clearly be central. But collaborative research is not necessarily non-hierarchical.

Some researchers have described how they have decided to use life history because of its potential to be a non-hierarchical approach. Their concern has been to abolish status and power differentials between researcher and informant (a central aim of those who advocate 'feminist' research). The sorts of interview-conversation used by life historians, together with the level of collaboration (in planning, data collection and analysis) that they can achieve with the approach can appear to offer the opportunity to engage in non-hierarchical, non-exploitative research. On this level, informants can be seen to be empowered as co-researchers. However, there can be a contradiction here. If life history is undertaken in order to 'give voice' to people who would not otherwise be heard, and if it is the life historian who is in the position of providing the channel to enable those voices to be heard, then there is an inevitable inequality.

When, as has frequently been the case, life history is used with informants who have relatively little social power then, it seems to us, there is an inherent status differential. It is also the case that, by and large, professional researchers will have specialist knowledge and expertise that informants do not possess. Munro (1998) has written about the way in which her desire that her work should be collaborative and non-hierarchical was disappointed because her informants (she called them 'life historians') did not consider their role to demand the level of involvement she wished for. Pat (Sikes 1997) also experienced this in her Parents Who Teach project. Maybe the dilemma is more semantic than anything else. There are numerous social hierarchies, and ensuring total match is perhaps unrealistic (although there are those who do argue for symmetry in research relationships). The most important – and the ethical – requirement should surely be, simply, for researchers to respect their informants and to treat them in a proper and moral fashion.

Further considerations

Any discussion around the issue of emancipation and empowerment through research assumes that informants lack social power. To a considerable extent this has tended to be the case and there are very few studies (using any kind of methodology) of elite groups. Elites tend to guard their position jealously and it is often not in their interests to have their beliefs, values, behaviours and practices widely known. Consequently, they are less likely to agree to participate, and when they do, they may present a very guarded, or even 'untrue' account. For example, in their life history work with members of the educational policy elite, Jenny Ozga and Sharon Gewirtz (1994) noted that, owing to the nature of their jobs and the power they possessed, their informants were particularly skilled and experienced in self-presentation and were 'very aware of their place in the narrative they constructed' (Ozga 2000).

Perhaps life historians have an ethical responsibility to ensure that they do try to work with a wider spectrum of society. However, saying this raises yet another ethical issue around whether or not it is morally right to give voice, through life history research, to anyone and everyone. We have just noted that it could be empowering to the public at large to conduct research with privileged and protected groups. What about those individuals and groups who hold beliefs or engage in actions which are in some way socially unacceptable or even illegal? If placed in the position of informants, they may take advantage of the opportunity to offer a justification for themselves. Plummer (1995), for instance, discusses how some paedophiles have attempted to create an alternative regime of truth by telling a positive story about their actions and desires without denying that they wanted to have sex with children (see also Sikes 2000a).

One response might be that research with people who potentially pose a threat to others (for example sex offenders, fascists, racists, burglars, embezzlers) is useful because it allows us to begin to understand them and their operations, and therefore we can better protect ourselves. Indeed, this is the line frequently taken by the media who often present life-history-type documentaries of such individuals. However, it seems that there is an ethical issue here which researchers do need to consider.

This chapter has focused on the ethical responsibility of the researcher to their informants. This is because researchers are the anticipated audience. However, it is worth pointing out that, sometimes, researchers are on the receiving end of unethical treatment by informants. That this is the case rather shifts the status differential – and raises issues around the notion of collaborative research. If research is truly collaborative then both parties have the same responsibilities to each other. It would be unethical if a researcher took advantage, in any way, of their informant. The relationship has to be a professional one, conducted according to professional codes. Researchers have to think about what they will do if they find themselves in a difficult situation: usually they should withdraw. Pat once had the experience of working with a young teacher who was apparently very keen to be involved in a research project. The interview-conversations proceeded satisfactorily and, from Pat's point of view, a good professional relationship had been established, until the teacher tried (unsuccessfully) to involve her in a pyramid selling organization. Pat felt very used – and even more so when, a few years after, she watched a TV programme about the entrapment methods used by this company and realized that she had been fed the classic lines.

Then there are, unfortunately and perhaps inevitably, those occasions where sexual advances are made by the informant to the researcher. We mention this because it does happen and people should be aware of the possibility and guard against finding themselves in a potentially dangerous situation. By and large, this means treating life history interviews with the same degree of caution that you would exercise in any other social encounter: thus, do not meet people in lonely or deserted places and let someone else know where you are going. Life historians are often concerned to ensure that the physical circumstances in which they conduct their work are comfortable and relaxing and it is quite usual to offer to go to someone's house. Without wishing to be alarmist, this does introduce an element of risk – again, something that is rarely mentioned in research texts.

As we said at the start of this chapter, any research involves ethical considerations. Our aim has been to alert readers to some of the areas of ethical concern likely to be encountered by life historians as they go about their work. Above all, we claim not that life history resolves or avoids ethical issues, rather that life history can be a rather permeable method, allowing greater transparency, in issues of values and ethics. As always, a method can have such potential, but delivery depends on those involved in the life history transaction. The devil is in the details of these interactions and transactions, for these are the heartland of ethical mediation.

7 | Confronting the dilemmas

Introduction

In writing this book we have been concerned to emphasize that relationships, selves and identities are central to all facets of the research process, whatever approach is used.

In the introduction to her book *The Ethnographic Self*, Amanda Coffey explains how her focus is on:

> the relationships between the self and ethnographic fieldwork . . . the idea behind the book is that ethnographers (and others involved in fieldwork research) should be aware of how fieldwork research and textual practice, construct, reproduce and implicate selves, relationships and personal identities.
>
> (Coffey 1999: 1)

It may be, though, that life history, even more so than ethnography, forces the researcher to acknowledge the personal and emotional aspects of their work for themselves, for their informants, and for those who read or otherwise access their research and accounts or productions. And it is these aspects which constitute the substance of the various dilemmas which have to be confronted if research integrity is to be maintained. These dilemmas are not in any way unique to life history. Nor can they be regarded as discrete categories of dilemma: interrelationships abound. However, in order to provide a framework for comprehension, this is how they will be presented here.

The dilemmas

Dilemmas to do with choosing to take a life history approach in the first place

'The positivist and postpositivist traditions linger like long shadows over the qualitative research project' (Denzin and Lincoln 1994b: 5), and continue to cast their shade at the start of the twenty-first century. However vociferously we may argue the case for qualitative research, Troyna's comment that, 'the question of credibility is one which, unfortunately, cannot be wished away' (Troyna 1994: 9) still holds. Adopting a methodological approach which deals with, and indeed celebrates, subjectivities, means choosing an approach whose status and respectability are regarded as dubious by many individuals, organizations and institutions whose power means that their opinions can matter.

We have argued earlier in the text that modernist methodologies have succumbed to a range of 'objectivity tests' by which to earn status and prestige. This is not unrelated to the various complicities by which research is integrated into the overall gaze of power. 'Objectivity' abstracts and aggregates the research scrutiny of the social order, thereby burying the subjective implications of sociopolitical processes. As illustrated in Chapter 1, the move to present sociology as an objective science led to a decline in life history work and to a consequent muzzling of the qualitative appraisal of subjective experience: so, not to put too fine a point on it, using life history can have negative implications for a researcher's career development. It may make it harder to achieve academic qualifications, to get work published and therefore read; to attract funding and to attain seniority and promotion, even though the 'objective' status of quantitative and 'scientific' research is no longer as inviolate as it once was. In fact, it has been suggested that one important reason why women have apparently been more willing to embrace auto/biographical and narrative forms is that they have less to lose (see, for example, Grumet 1991; Cotterill and Letherby 1993; Emihovitch 1995; Sikes 1997).

Whether or not this is the case, life historians who want their work to reach the wider community do frequently have to construct an especially strong and strident justification and defence for their methodology, in a climate where the positivist paradigm maintains its hegemony – although for how long is another matter for as Clandinin and Connelly (1990: 252) have defiantly claimed: 'neither the hegemonies of form nor the constraints of maxim and rule, nor even the bonds of autobiography, are safe from the reconstructions of narrative'.

Dilemmas to do with the relationship between individual lives and social settings

Life historians have to acknowledge the complexity of the relationship between the individual and society, especially with regard to the ways in which people tell their stories and locate their lives. The extent to which this is a dilemma depends on the aims of any particular study. If the intention is to take and to present a purely phenomenological (rather than life historical) perspective, any individual account will be adequate. However, this line assumes that people do have sufficient knowledge to explain everything about their lives and what they do. Yet, because of such things as differential social positioning and the workings of the sub- and unconscious mind, this is unlikely to be the case (see Bhaskar 1989; Maynard and Purvis 1994). As Rosen comments:

> A person's knowledge can only exist by virtue of a vast range of experiences which have been lived through, often with the most intense feelings. These experiences, including textual experiences (books, lectures, lessons, conversations etc), we have been taught to disguise so that our utterances are made to seem as though they emerge from no particular place or time or person but from the fount of knowledge itself.
>
> (Rosen 1998: 30)

Rosen is pointing to the recursive nature of social life which has particular pertinence for the life historian, as David Scott emphasizes when he suggests that:

> the most compelling problem then for social portrayists is the precise relationship between structure and agency, which is of course an ontological matter, and then between this relationship and the biographer, which on the surface seems to be purely an epistemological matter. However, the precise epistemological mode becomes an ontological matter since the text produced has real material effects, albeit in discursive form.
>
> (Scott 1998: 33)

Our approach to this problem lies in differentiating the life *story* from the life *history* (Goodson 1992a), and in the way in which the *history* supplies both contexts in which to locate the *story* and frameworks for interpreting it. In this way it is possible to gain some glimpse of, and insight into, the rupture and the marriage between individual lives and the social settings in which they are lived.

Dilemmas to do with the 'power' of informants vis-à-vis
researchers

The authors of method texts tend to assume that, unless working with members of elite groups, the balance of power in research relationships lies with the researcher. Undoubtedly, in many instances and with regard to many aspects of research relationships and processes, this is the case, and all researchers should give detailed consideration to ethical issues and be alert to the dangers. The nature of life history methodology and the 'data' it yields requires particular sensitivity, and throughout this book we have tried to alert readers to some of the hidden, as well as the more obvious, potential pitfalls. Thus, we have discussed how the use of standard research techniques such as reciprocity needs careful thought if it is not to be simply a means of manipulation and exploitation for the sake of 'better' data. We have also considered the complexity and problematical aspects of claims to emancipate and empower 'silenced lives' through 'giving voice'. The overriding message is of the responsibility to maintain a reflective and reflexive stance because, regardless of any status differentials between researcher and informant, possessing personal life story data inevitably confers power and, therefore, the potential to do damage.

We implied at the start of this section that the power is not all or always in favour of the researcher. All discussions about the validity, reliability, veracity, truth, verisimilitude (and so on) of subjective data are founded on the acknowledgement, if not the expectation, that informants may deliberately and consciously lie (see Sikes 2000a). Successful lies will never be found out. Inevitably, and definitely where practice is ethical, decisions regarding whether to participate in the research and, if so, what should be disclosed, ultimately rest with informants. Looked at from this perspective, informants actually have considerable power to influence whether the research takes place, not to mention their control over what is available as data. Our contention throughout, though, has been that life history is a relatively 'permeable' method where transparency over issues of procedure and ethics is maximized. More 'objective' methods, often in the name of scientific truth, obscure some of these aspects: by hiding subjective experience, a different form of obfuscation (a displaced form of lying, even) is practised.

Dilemmas to do with the informants' involvement

It seems likely that, for the majority of people who get involved in life history research as informants, there are no long term or significant implications or repercussions. People frequently comment that they enjoyed the chance to talk about themselves and the opportunity to reflect on experiences, but apart perhaps from giving them a positive, participative view of research and a sense of contributing to academic endeavour, that is about it. For a small minority though, being involved in a life history project can have life-changing effects. Sometimes this is the intention as, for instance, when life history workshops are held for professional development purposes. On other occasions the consequences are unexpected. Relating and reflecting on one's life and doing life history, contextualizing work can lead to new insights and perspectives that may find their ultimate expression in some sort of change. This change may be minor in terms of its objective consequences, but in some cases it can be substantial.

Engaging in life history work can sometimes be painful in that informants may find themselves revisiting distressing events. Some informants may be quite prepared to do this because remembering such events has become part of their everyday lives; for others the experience may be shocking, disturbing and unexpected. Life historians need to have thought about the potential implications that being involved in their research has for their informants. Although effects cannot easily be predicted, the fact remains that being involved in life history work can alter lives.

Dilemmas to do with presentation

Each stage in the telling, hearing and re-presenting of life stories and the work that is done in turning them into life histories can be seen as taking the account that bit further away from the life as lived. It can never be possible to tell, capture or present an actual life: any attempt will be mediated by language and by the interpretative frames through which it is both presented and made sense of. In other words, because of my personal experiences, perceptions, beliefs, social positioning, historical and geographical location and so on, I will make sense of a life hi/story in (at least) a slightly different way from you. This is the case, whoever 'you' and 'I' happen to be. There are, of course, certain universals and much common ground, but ultimately and inevitably there will be differences. When it comes to writing up and presenting life histories, these differences can become problematical because the question arises of whose hi/story the researcher is presenting, whose interpretations, whose truths are given primacy?

Then there are the consequences and implications of presenting lives in a particular way, not least of which is the way in which life stories are consumed by people who then compare and contrast their own lives with them. With regard to this point, there are dialogical implications and consequences for future biographers and life historians, because their informants may well be influenced to tell their lives in particular ways, by prior scripts and storylines promoted by previous studies.

Once again, our advice is to reflect carefully on the issues and to acknowledge explicitly the position that is finally adopted when it comes to presentation and publication.

Alternative lives

At various points throughout this book we have talked about the ways in which life stories and life histories can help people to understand their own and others' lives; can validate choices, lifestyles and ways of being; can show how others have dealt with similar experiences, and so on. They can do this for researchers, informants, readers and hearers alike. Any life hi/story work also raises the ghost of alternative lives, the haunting 'what ifs' and 'if onlys' that would have made all the difference. Over the years, talking with informants, friends, family, colleagues and, especially, with each other, we have both become fascinated by the notion of alternative lives and have come to the view that they are worthy of consideration in their own right.

After tragedies people often say, 'if only such and such, then the disaster wouldn't have happened'. Death obviously pre-empts possibilities and opportunities for the deceased and also for those who might have encountered them. Being born into a particular family, in a particular place at a particular time, and possessing particular physical, mental and emotional capabilities, puts us on particular life trajectories which can be difficult to resist. Going to that particular school, marrying that particular person, meeting that particular mentor, and so on, all have particular outcomes contingent upon their particular character.

As the scholarship boy stories quoted earlier demonstrated, education has traditionally and formally been used a means of interrupting selected lives and setting them down alternative paths. Other ruptures, though, result from happenstance and serendipity. Yet, however the changes were instigated, people who have experienced significant changes from the course their life might have been expected to take, often live within the shadow of what might have been. The shadow is there for all of us, and we can learn a considerable amount about ourselves and aspects of society from speculating on possible alternatives. Earlier in the book, the story of Hillary and Matthew gave some indication of the possible personal consequences of 'if onlys'. For Pat Sikes, a working-class girl, going to school in the 1960s in Leicestershire meant (among other things) a comprehensive education, an open-access sixth-form, and a rich cultural and, especially, musical education. Had she lived in the city, she would have been required to take the 11-plus examination, would probably have failed, gone to a secondary modern school, not met Lawrence Stenhouse and would definitely not have a PhD and be working in a university. That is only a cursory example, but even so it has a lot to tell about educational organization, gender, social class and the importance of sponsorship by mentors.

These experiences of alternative stories and marginalities are central to the understandings of the authors of this book. As for Pat Sikes, Ivor Goodson's experience of working-class life provided endless episodes of the future as 'scripted' for children of manual labourers. Hence, having failed eight out of nine O-levels at age 15, he found himself at work with a group of his local friends in a potato chip factory. Working from 7am until 6.30pm, the future looked fairly predictable. But let us revert to story mode:

> One day I was having my sandwiches in the works canteen during the half-hour lunch break. As I looked up, I noticed a familiar face in the canteen coming towards me, carrying a cup of tea.
> I was amazed to realise that it was my old history teacher from the grammar school. What was he doing there?
> 'Can I join you?'
> 'Sure.'
> 'What are you doing here?' I asked.
> 'Well, I popped in to see Dyos (the chemistry teacher who worked as a consultant testing some of the processing), and so I thought I'd look for you . . . since you did so well in your 'O' levels!' (History was the *only* subject I passed.)
> 'So here I am'
> 'What's it like?'
> 'The truth . . . it's f. . .g terrible.' (First time I'd sworn in front of a teacher.)
> We paused, sat in silence for a bit.
> 'Why don't you come back to school . . . you're bright enough?'
> Further pause.
> 'Well, I might just do that.'

In the event, Ivor went back to school and this time began passing his exams. Three years later, again with this teacher's help and guidance, he was studying at London University. The story is, therefore, similar to Pat's, and explains an enduring fascination with alternative lives.

Constructing alternative life histories is similar to, but at the same time different from, taking a fictional narrative. The similarities lie in the stories and in the nature of stories.

> We live in worlds cluttered with material hurdles, the everyday pains of our sedimented histories, but the best stories help us to see where we are and move on . . . (for all story) cycles end with the chance of a new beginning, an opportunity to play the cycle through differently, with different outcomes. You listen to the story to imagine what else might be possible.
>
> (Battacharya 1998)

The difference lies in what we know about our own possibilities and what the alternatives might have meant for us.

Finally

In his autobiography, the artist-craftsman Eric Gill (1940) wrote, not very convincingly, it has to be said, 'nothing very particular has happened to me – except inside my head'. Coming from such a vital, creative and controversial figure as Gill, such a comment is worthy of detailed deconstruction (for which this is not the place). Gill's various biographers took a slightly different line and, whilst accepting that what went on inside the man's head was incredibly and undoubtedly significant, located his story, his perceptions, his work, within the relevant wider social, artistic, religious, sexual (and so on) contexts. Such location provides insights into, and ways of making sense of: (1) Gill's extraordinary and unique work and lifestyle, the impact and influence he had on others in various spheres of life; and (2) his personal perceptions and understandings. Those engaged in life history, whether as researchers, informants or readers/consumers are involved in much the same endeavour, seeking to interpret and re-present the world, or more precisely, aspects of the social world, through a method which explicitly acknowledges and is based on the belief that social and personal 'realities' originate in the dialogical relationship between individuals and groups and the values and practices which characterize social worlds.

We find life history fascinating and fun. We like doing it and we enjoy reading it. Like W. Thomas, C. Wright Mills and Herbert Blumer (among others), we believe that it has a prominent place in social science methodology. We hope that through this book we have managed to convey why we hold these views and, most importantly, we hope that we have persuaded readers to undertake their own life history work. By stressing throughout the personal involvement and pleasure we find in life history study, we have tried to show how such work can add passion and purpose to social science.

Bibliography

Abbs, P. (1974) *Autobiography in Education*. London: Heinemann.

Altheide, D. and Johnson, J. (1994) Criteria for assessing interpretive validity in qualitative research, in N. Denzin and Y. Lincoln (eds) *Handbook of Qualitative Research*, pp. 485–99. London: Sage.

Anderson, N. (1923) *The Hobo*. Chicago: University of Chicago Press.

Aspinwall, K. (1986) Teacher biography: the in-service potential, *Cambridge Journal of Education*, 16: 210–15.

Atkinson, P. (1990) *The Ethnographic Imagination*. London: Routledge.

Attwood, M. (1996) *Alias Grace*. London: Bloomsbury.

Bakhtin, M. (1981) *The Dialogic Imagination*. Austin, TX: University of Texas Press.

Ball, S. (1990) Self doubt and soft data: social and technical trajectories in ethnographic fieldwork, *International Journal of Qualitative Studies in Education*, 3(2): 151–71.

Ball, S. and Goodson, I. (eds) (1985) *Teachers' Lives and Careers*. London: Falmer Press.

Banks, A. and Banks, S. (eds) (1998) *Fiction and Social Research: By Ice or Fire*. Walnut Creek, CA: AltaMira.

Baronne, T. (1995) Persuasive writings, vigilant readings, and reconstructed characters: the paradox of trust in educational storytelling, in J. Hatch and R. Wisniewski (eds) *Life History and Narrative*, pp. 63–74. London: Falmer Press.

Barrett, S. (1906) *Geronimo's Story of His Life: Taken Down and Edited by S.M. Barrett*. New York: Duffield.

Bascia, N. (1996) Making sense of the lives and work of racial minority immigrant teachers, in D. Thiessen, N. Bascia and I. Goodson (eds) *Making a Difference About Difference: The Lives and Careers of Racial Minority Immigrant Teachers*, pp. 1–14. Canada: REMTEL/Garamond.

Battacharya, G. (1998) *Tales of Dark-skinned Women*. London: University College.

Becker, H. (1970) *Sociological Work: Method and Substance*. Chicago: Aldine.

Berger, P. (1963) *Invitation to Sociology*. Garden City, NY: Doubleday.

Berger, P. and Luckmann, T. (1967) *The Social Construction of Reality*. Garden City, NY: Anchor Books.

Bertaux, D. (1981) *Biography and Society: The Life History Approach in the Social Sciences*. London: Sage.

Bhaskar, R. (1989) *Reclaiming Reality*. London: Verso.

Blaxter, L., Hughes, C. and Tight, M. (1999) *How to Research*. Buckingham: Open University Press.

Blunkett, D. (2000) Influence or Irrelevance: Can Social Science Improve Government? Speech to ESRC, *Research Intelligence*, 71: 12–21.

Bogdan, R. (1974) *Being Different: The Autobiography of Jane Fry*. New York: Wiley.

Bridges, D. (1999) Faction and friction: educational narrative research and the 'magic of the real'. Unpublished paper.

Bruner, J. (1986) *Actual Minds, Possible Worlds*. Cambridge, MA: Harvard University Press.

Bruner, J. (1990) *Acts of Meaning*. Cambridge, MA: Harvard University Press.

Bullough, R. (1989) *First Year Teacher*. New York: Teachers College Press.

Bullough, R. (1998) Musings on life writing: biography and case study in teacher education, in C. Kridel (ed.) *Writing Educational Biography: Explorations in Qualitative Research*, pp. 19–32. New York: Garland.

Bullough, R. and Baughman, K. (1997) *A Teacher's Journey: First Year Teacher Revisited*. New York: Teachers College Press.

Bullough, R., Knowles, G. and Crow, N. (1991) *Emerging as a Teacher*. London: Routledge.

Butt, R., Raymond, D., McCue, G. and Yamagishi, L. (1992) Collaborative autobiography and the teacher's voice, in I. Goodson (ed.) *Studying Teachers' Lives*, pp. 51–98. London: Routledge.

Casey, K. (1993) *I Answer With My Life: Life Histories of Women Teachers Working for Social Change*. New York: Routledge.

Chambliss, W. (1972) *Boxman: A Professional Thief*. New York: Harper & Row.

Clandinin, D. and Connelly, F. (1990) Narrative, experience and the study of curriculum, *Cambridge Journal of Education*, 20(3): 241–53.

Clandinin, D. and Connelly, F. (1994) Personal experience methods, in N. Denzin and Y. Lincoln (eds) *Handbook of Qualitative Research*, pp. 413–27. London: Sage.

Clandinin, D. and Connelly, F. (1998) Asking questions about telling stories, in C. Kridel (ed.) *Writing Educational Biography: Explorations in Qualitative Research*, pp. 245–53. New York: Garland.

Clough, P. (1992) *The End(s) of Ethnography*. London: Sage.

Clough, P. (1999) Crises of schooling and the 'crisis of representation': the story of Rob, *Qualitative Inquiry*, 5(3): 428–48.

Coffey, A. (1999) *The Ethnographic Self: Fieldwork and the Representation of Identity*. London: Sage.

Cornwell, C. and Sutherland, E. (1937) *The Professional Thief*. Chicago: University of Chicago Press.

Cosslett, T. (1994) *Women Writing Childbirth: Modern Discourses of Motherhood*. Manchester: Manchester University Press.

Cotterill, P. and Letherby, G. (1993) Weaving stories: personal auto/biographies in feminist research, *Sociology*, 27(1): 67–80.

Cuff, E. and Payne, G. (1979) *Perspectives in Sociology*. London: Allen & Unwin.

Dannefer, D. (1992) On the conceptualization of context in developmental discourse: four meanings of context and their implications, in D. Featherman, R. Lerner, M. Perlmutter (eds) *Life-span Development and Behaviour*, 11: 84–110. Hillsdale, NJ: Lawrence Erlbaum Associates.

Denscombe, M. (1984) Interviews, accounts and ethnography: research on teachers, in M. Hammersley (ed.) *The Ethnography of Schooling*, pp. 107–28. Driffield: Nafferton.

Denscombe, M. (1998) *The Good Research Guide for Small-scale Social Research Projects*. Buckingham: Open University Press.

Denzin, N. (1970) *The Research Act in Sociology: A Theoretical Introduction to Sociological Methods*. Chicago: Aldine.

Denzin, N. (1997) *Interpretive Ethnography: Ethnographic Practices for the 21st Century*. London: Sage.

Denzin, N. and Lincoln, Y. (eds) (1994a) *Handbook of Qualitative Research*. London: Sage.

Denzin, N. and Lincoln, Y. (1994b) Introduction: Entering the field of qualitative research, in N. Denzin and Y. Lincoln (eds) *Handbook of Qualitative Research*, pp. 1–18. London: Sage.

Denzin, N. and Lincoln, Y. (eds) (2000) *Handbook of Qualitative Research*, 2nd edn. Thousand Oaks, CA: Sage.

Dollard, J. (1949) *Criteria for the Life History*. Magnolia, MA: Peter Smith.

Douglas, C. (1998) The people's frail healer, *Guardian*, 25 June, p. 4.

Draper, T. (1993) Iran-Contra: the mystery solved, *New York Review of Books*, XL(11) (10 June).

Dygregrov, A. and Dygregrov, K. (1999) Long term impact of sudden infant death: 12–15 year follow up, *Death Studies*, 23(V): 635–61.

Elbaz, F. (1983) *Teacher Thinking: A Study of Practical Knowledge*. London: Croom Helm.

Ellis, C. and Bochner, A. (2000) Autoethnography, personal narrative, reflexivity, in N. Denzin and Y. Lincoln (eds) *Handbook of Qualitative Research*, 2nd edn, pp. 733–68, Thousand Oaks, CA: Sage.

Emihovitch, C. (1995) Distancing passion: narratives in social science, in J. Hatch and R. Wisniewski (eds) *Life History and Narrative*, pp. 37–48. London: Falmer Press.

Erben, M. (1998a) Introduction, in M. Erben (ed.) *Biography and Education: A Reader*, pp. 1–3. London: Falmer Press.

Erben, M. (1998b) Biography and research methods, in M. Erben (ed.) *Biography and Education: A Reader*, pp. 4–17. London: Falmer Press.

Faris, R. (1967) *Chicago Sociology*. San Francisco. Chandler

Fine, M. (1994) Working the hyphens: reinventing self and other in qualitative research, in N. Denzin and Y. Lincoln (eds) *Handbook of Qualitative Research*, pp. 70–82. London: Sage.

Fitzclarence, L. (1991) 'Remembering the reconceptualist project'. Paper presented at the Bergamo Conference, Dayton, Ohio, October.

Fontana, F. and Frey, J. (1994) Interviewing: the art of science, in N. Denzin and Y. Lincoln (eds) *Handbook of Qualitative Research*, pp. 361–76. London: Sage.

Freeman, M. (1993) *Rewriting the Self: History, Memory, Narrative*. London: Routledge.

Gergen, K. (1991) *The Saturated Self: Dilemmas of Identity in Contemporary Life.* New York: Basic Books.

Gill, E. (1940) *Autobiography.* London: Cape.

Giroux, H. (1991) *Border Crossings.* London: Routledge & Kegan Paul.

Gluck, S. and Patai, D. (eds) (1991) *Women's Words: The Feminist Practice of Oral History.* New York: Routledge.

Goodson, I. (1981) Life histories and the study of schooling, *Interchange*, 11(4): 62–75.

Goodson, I. (1983) Life histories and teaching, in M. Hammersley (ed.) *The Ethnography of Schooling.* Driffield: Nafferton.

Goodson, I. (1991) Sponsoring the teacher's voice: teachers' lives and teacher development, *Cambridge Journal of Education*, 21(1): 35–45.

Goodson, I. (ed.) (1992a) *Studying Teachers' Lives.* London: Routledge.

Goodson, I. (1992b) Studying teachers' lives: an emergent field of enquiry, in I. Goodson (ed.) *Studying Teachers' Lives*, pp. 1–17. London: Routledge.

Goodson, I. (1992c) Studying teachers' lives: problems and possibilities, in I. Goodson (ed.) *Studying Teachers' Lives*, pp. 234–49. London: Routledge.

Goodson, I. (1995) The story so far: personal knowledge and the political, in J. Hatch and R. Wisniewski (eds) *Life History and Narrative*, pp. 89–98. London: Falmer Press.

Goodson, I. (1997) *The Changing Curriculum: Studies in Social Construction.* Bonn: Peter Lang.

Goodson, I. (2000) 'Collecting life stories'. Paper presented at the University of East Anglia summer conference.

Goodson, I. (2001) *Professional Knowledge: Educational Studies and the Teacher.* Buckingham: Open University Press.

Goodson, I. and Fliesser, C. (1994) Exchanging gifts: collaborative research and theories of context, *Analytic Teaching*, 15(2): 41–6.

Goodson, I. and Fliesser, C. (1995) Negotiating fair trade: towards collaborative relationships between researchers and teachers in college settings, *Peabody Journal of Education*, 70(3): 5–17.

Goodson, I. and Hargreaves, A. (1996) *Teachers' Professional Lives.* London: Falmer Press.

Goodson, I. and Mangan, J.M. (1995) Developing a collaborative research strategy with teachers for the study of classroom computing, *Journal of Information Technology for Teacher Education*, 4(3): 269–87.

Goodson, I. and Walker, R. (1991) *Biography, Identity and Schooling: Episodes in Educational Research.* London: Falmer Press.

Goodson, I., Mangan, J.M., Lankshear, C. and Knobel, M. (2001) *Computer Wars.* New York: St Martin's Press.

Griffiths, M. (1998) *Educational Research for Social Justice: Getting Off the Fence.* Buckingham: Open University Press.

Grumet, M. (1981) Restitution and reconstruction of educational experience: an autobiographical method for curriculum theory, in M. Lawn and L. Barton (eds) *Rethinking Curriculum Studies*, pp. 115–30. London: Croom Helm.

Grumet, M. (1991) The politics of personal knowledge, in C. Withering and N. Nodding (eds) *Stories Lives Tell: Narrative and Dialogue in Education*, pp. 66–77. New York: Teachers College Press.

Gullette, M. (1988) *Safe at Last in the Middle Years*. Berkeley, CA: University of California Press.

Hammersley, M. (2000) *Taking Sides in Social Research: Essays on Partisanship and Bias*. London: Routledge.

Hampl, P. (1996) Memory and imagination, in J. McConkey (ed.) *The Anatomy of Memory: An Anthology*, pp. 201–11. New York: Oxford University Press.

Hargreaves, D. (1996) Teaching as a research-based profession: possibilities and prospects. Teacher Training Agency Annual Lecture, London.

Harvey, D. (1989) *The Condition of Postmodernity*. London: Blackwell.

Hatch, J.A. and Wisniewski, R. (eds) (1995) *Life History and Narrative*. London: Falmer Press.

Haug, F. (1999) *Female Sexualization: A Collective Work of Memory*, trans. E. Carter. London: Verso.

Hepworth, M. (2000) *Stories of Ageing*. Buckingham: Open University Press.

Hoerning, E. (1985) Upward mobility and family estrangement among females: what happens when the 'same old girl' becomes the 'new professional woman'? *International Journal of Oral History*, 6(2): 107–14.

Hoggart, R. (1958) *The Uses of Literacy*. Harmondsworth: Penguin (in association with Chatto & Windus).

Holly, M. (1989) *Writing to Grow: Keeping a Personal-Professional Journal*. Portsmouth, NH: Heinemann.

Huberman, M. (1993) *The Lives of Teachers*, trans. J. Neufeld. London: Cassell.

Humphries, L. (1970) *Tearoom Trade*. Chicago: Aldine.

Joannou, M. (1995) 'She who would be politically free herself must strike the blow': suffragette autobiography and suffragette militancy, in J. Swindells (ed.) *The Uses of Autobiography*, pp. 31–44. London: Taylor & Francis.

Johnson, G. (1993) Eight interviews carried out between 11 January and 26 October.

Josselson, R. (1995) Imagining the real: empathy, narrative and the dialogic self, in R. Josselson and A. Lieblich (eds) *Interpreting Experience*, pp. 27–44. Thousand Oaks, CA: Sage.

Klockars, C. (1975) *The Professional Fence*. London: Tavistock.

Kridel, C. (ed.) (1998) *Writing Educational Biography: Explorations in Qualitative Research*. New York: Garland.

Lather, P. (1986) Research as praxis, *Harvard Educational Review*, 56(3): 257–77.

Lee, N. and Renzetti, M. (1993) The problems of researching sensitive topics: an overview, in M. Renzetti and N. Lee (eds) *Researching Sensitive Topics*, pp. 3–13. London: Sage.

Levinson, D. (1979) *The Seasons of a Man's Life*. New York: Ballantine.

Lincoln, Y. and Denzin, N. (1994) The fifth moment, in N. Denzin and Y. Lincoln (eds) *Handbook of Qualitative Research*, pp. 575–86. London: Sage.

Lincoln, Y. and Guba, E. (1985) *Naturalistic Inquiry*. New York: Sage.

Lincoln, Y. and Guba, E. (1989) Ethics: the failure of positivist science, *Review of Higher Education*, 12: 221–4.

Maynard, M. (1993) Feminism and the possibilities of a postmodern research practice, *British Journal of Sociology of Education*, 14(3): 327–31.

Maynard, M. and Purvis, J. (1994) Doing feminist research, in M. Maynard and J. Purvis (eds) *Researching Women's Lives From a Feminist Perspective*, pp. 1–9. London: Taylor & Francis.

McLaughlin, D. and Tierney, W. (eds) (1993) *Naming Silent Lives: Personal Narratives and Processes of Educational Change.* New York: Routledge.

Measor, L. and Sikes, P. (1992) Visiting lives: ethics and methodology in life history research, in I. Goodson (ed.) *Studying Teachers' Lives*, pp. 209–33. London: Routledge.

Middleton, S. (1992) Developing a radical pedagogy: autobiography of a New Zealand sociologist of women's education, in I. Goodson (ed.) *Studying Teachers' Lives*, pp. 18–50. London: Routledge.

Middleton, S. (1993) *Educating Feminists: Life Histories and Pedagogy.* New York: Teachers College Press/London: Sage.

Middleton, S. (1997) *Disciplining Sexuality: Foucault, Life Histories and Education.* New York: Teachers College Press.

Milgram, S. (1963) Behavioural study of obedience, *Journal of Abnormal and Social Psychology*, 67: 371–8.

Miller, R. (2000) *Researching Life Stories and Family Histories.* London: Sage.

Mitchell, C. and Weber, S. (1999) *Reinventing Ourselves as Teachers: Beyond Nostalgia.* London: Falmer Press.

Morris, M. (1977) *An Excursion into Creative Sociology.* New York: Columbia University Press.

Morse, J. (1994) Designing funded qualitative research, in N. Denzin and Y. Lincoln (eds) *Handbook of Qualitative Research*, pp. 220–35. London: Sage.

Munro, P. (1998) *Subject to Fiction: Women Teachers' Life History Narratives and the Cultural Politics of Resistance.* Buckingham: Open University Press.

Nielsen, J. (ed.) (1990) *Feminist Research Methods: Exemplary Readings in the Social Sciences.* London: Westview Press.

Oakley, A. (1979) *From Here to Maternity: Becoming a Mother.* Harmondsworth: Penguin.

Oakley, A. (1981) Interviewing women: a contradiction in terms, in H. Roberts (ed.) *Doing Feminist Research*, pp. 30–61. London: Routledge & Kegan Paul.

Osler, A. (1997) *The Education and Careers of Black Teachers: Changing Identities, Changing Lives.* Buckingham: Open University Press.

Ozga, J. (2000) *Policy Research in Educational Settings: Contested Terrain.* Buckingham: Open University Press.

Ozga, J. and Gewirtz, S. (1994) Sex, lies and audiotape: interviewing the education policy elite, in D. Halpin and B. Troyna (eds) *Researching Education Policy: Ethical and Methodological Issues*, pp. 121–36. London: Falmer Press.

Passerini, L. (1987) *Fascism in Popular Memory: The Cultural Experience of the Turin Working Class.* Cambridge: Cambridge University Press.

Personal Narratives Group (eds) (1989) *Interpreting Women's Lives: Feminist Theory and Personal Narratives.* Bloomington, IN: Indiana University Press.

Peters, W. (1987) *A Class Divided: Then and Now.* New Haven, CT: Yale University Press.

Phoenix, A. (1994) Practising feminist research: the intersection of gender and 'race' in the research process, in M. Maynard and J. Purvis (eds) *Researching Women's Lives from a Feminist Perspective*, pp. 49–71. London: Taylor & Francis.

Pinar, W. (1994) *Autobiography, Politics and Sexuality.* New York: Peter Lang.

Plummer, K. (1983) *Documents of Life.* London: Allen & Unwin.

Plummer, K. (1990) Herbert Blumer and the life history tradition, *Symbolic Interactionism*, 13: 125–44.

Plummer, K. (1995) *Telling Sexual Stories: Power, Change and Social Worlds*. London: Routledge.

Polkinghorne, D. (1988) *Narrative Knowing and the Human Sciences*. Albany, NY: State University of New York Press.

Powney, J. and Watts, M. (1987) *Interviewing in Educational Research*. London: Routledge & Kegan Paul.

Quicke, J. (1988) Using structured life histories to teach the sociology and social psychology of education: an evaluation, in P. Woods and A. Pollard (eds) *Sociology and Teaching: A New Challenge for the Sociology of Education*, pp. 92–116. Beckenham: Croom Helm.

Radin, I. (1920) *Crashing Thunder*, Publications in Archaeology and Ethnology, Vol. 26, pp. 381–473.

Rakhit, A. (1999) The career experiences of Asian women teachers: a life history approach. Unpublished PhD thesis, University of Warwick.

Rapport, N. (1999) Life with a hole, howl, hill, hull in it: Philip Larkin at life's crossroads, *Auto/Biography*, VII(1/2): 3–12.

Ricoeur, P. (1974) *The Conflict of Interpretations*. Evanston, IL: Northwestern University Press.

Ricoeur, P. (1981) *Hermeneutics and the Human Sciences*. Cambridge: Cambridge University Press.

Ricoeur, P. (1980) Narrative time, *Critical Enquiry*, 7(1): 160–80.

Roberts, B. (1999) Some thoughts on time perspectives and auto/biography, *Auto/Biography*, VII(1/2): 21–5.

Robson, C. (1993) *Real World Research*. Oxford: Blackwell.

Rosen, H. (1998) *Speaking From Memory: The Study of Autobiographical Discourse*. Stoke-on-Trent: Trentham.

Rosie, A. (1993) 'He's a liar, I'm afraid': truth and lies in a narrative account, *Sociology*, special edition, *Auto/Biography in Sociology*, 27(1): 144–52.

Samuel, R. (1989) Heroes below the hooves of history, *Independent*, 31 August, p. 23.

Scott, D. (1998) Fragments of a life: recursive dilemmas, in M. Erben (ed.) *Biography and Education: A Reader*, pp. 32–45. London: Falmer Press.

Shacklock, G. and Smyth, J. (eds) (1998) *Being Reflexive in Critical Educational and Social Research*. London: Falmer Press.

Shaw, C. (1930) *The Jack-Roller*. Chicago: University of Chicago Press.

Shotter, J. (1993) *Cultural Politics of Everyday Life: Social Constructionism, Rhetoric and Knowing of the Third Kind*. Toronto: University of Toronto Press.

Shotter, J. and Gergen, K. (1989) *Texts of Identity*, Inquiries in Social Construction Series, Vol. 2. London: Sage.

Sikes, P. (1986) The mid-career teacher: adaptation and motivation in a contracting secondary school system. Unpublished PhD thesis, University of Leeds.

Sikes, P. (1997) *Parents Who Teach: Stories From Home and From School*. London: Cassell.

Sikes, P. (2000a) 'Truth' and 'lies' revisited, *British Educational Research Journal*, 26(2): 257–70.

Sikes, P. (2000b) Dangerous liaisons? When male teachers and female pupils fall in love. Unpublished paper.

Sikes, P. and Aspinwall, K. (1992) Time to reflect: biographical study, personal insight, and professional development, in R. Young and A. Collin (eds) *Interpreting Career: Hermeneutical Studies of Lives in Context*, pp. 177–88. Westport, CN: Praeger.

Sikes, P. and Troyna, B. (1991) True stories: a case study in the use of life history in initial teacher education, *Educational Review*, 43(1): 3–16.

Sikes, P., Measor, L. and Woods, P. (1985) *Teachers' Careers: Crises and Continuities*. Lewes: Falmer Press.

Sikes, P., Troyna, B. and Goodson, I. (1996) Talking lives: a conversation about life history, *Taboo: The Journal of Culture and Education*, 1 (Spring): 35–54.

Skeggs, B. (1994) Situating the production of feminist ethnography, in M. Maynard and J. Purvis (eds) *Researching Women's Lives from a Feminist Perspective*, pp. 72–92. London: Taylor & Francis.

Smyth, J. (1982) A teacher development approach to bridging the practice-research gap, *Journal of Curriculum Studies*, 14(4): 331–42.

Sparkes, A. (1995) Physical education teachers and the search for self: two cases of structured denial, in N. Armstrong (ed.) *New Directions in Physical Education*, Vol. 3, pp. 157–78. London: Cassell.

Sparkes, A. (1994) Self, silence and invisibility as a beginning teacher: a life history of lesbian experience, *British Journal of Sociology of Education*, 15(1): 93–118.

Stanley, I.. (1990) *Feminist Praxis, Research Theory and Epistemology in Feminist Sociology*. London: Routledge.

Stanley, L. (1992) *The Auto/Biographical: The Theory and Practice of Feminist Auto/Biography*. Manchester: Manchester University Press.

Stone, L. (1987) *The Past and the Present Revisited*. London: Routledge & Kegan Paul.

Thiessen, D., Bascia, N. and Goodson, I. (eds) (1996) *Making a Difference About Difference: The Lives and Careers of Racial Minority Immigrant Teachers*. Toronto: Garamond.

Thomas, W. and Znaniecki, F. (1918–1920) *The Polish Peasant in Europe and America*, 2nd edn. Chicago: University of Chicago Press.

Thompson, P. (1978) *The Voices of the Past: Oral History*. Oxford: Oxford University Press.

Thompson, P. (1988) *The Voices of the Past: Oral History*, 2nd edn. Oxford: Oxford University Press.

Thrasher, F. (1928) *The Gang: A Study of 1313 Gangs in Chicago*. Chicago: University of Chicago Press.

Tierney, W. (1998) Life history's history: subjects foretold, *Qualitative Inquiry*, 4(1): 49–70.

Todorov, T. (1977) *The Poetics of Prose*. New York: Cornell University Press.

Troyna, B. (1994) 'Blind faith?' Empowerment and educational research, *International Studies in the Sociology of Education*, 4(1): 3–24.

Troyna, B. and Sikes, P. (1989) Putting the 'why' back into teacher education, *Forum*, 32(1): 25–6.

Usher, R. (1998) The story of the self: education, experience and autobiography, in M. Erben (ed.) *Biography and Education: A Reader*, pp. 18–31. London: Falmer Press.

Wagner-Martin, L. (1998) The issue of gender: continuing problems in biography, in C. Kridel (ed.) *Writing Educational Biography: Explorations in Qualitative Research*, pp. 89–102. New York: Garland.

Weber, S. and Mitchell, C. (1995) *That's Funny, You Don't Look Like a Teacher! Interrogating Images and Identity in Popular Culture*. London: Falmer Press.

Weiler, K. and Middleton, S. (eds) (1999) *Telling Women's Lives: Narrative Inquiries in the History of Women's Education*. Buckingham: Open University Press.

Weiner, W. and Rosenwald, G. (1993) A moment's monument: the psychology of keeping a journal, in R. Josselson and A. Leiblich (eds) *The Narrative Study of Lives*, pp. 30–58. Newbury Park, CA: Sage.

Wirth, L. (1928) *The Ghetto*. Chicago: University of Chicago Press.

Wittgenstein, L. (1953) *Philosophical Investigations*. Oxford: Blackwell.

Wolcott, H. (1983) Adequate schools and inadequate education: the life history of a sneaky kid, *Anthropology and Education Quarterly*, 14(1): 3–32.

Woods, P. (1985) Conversations with teachers: some aspects of life history method, *British Educational Research Journal*, 11(1): 13–26.

Woods, P. (1986) *Inside Schools: Ethnography in Educational Research*. London: Routledge & Kegan Paul.

Woods, P. (1996) *Researching the Art of Teaching: Ethnography for Educational Use*. London: Routledge.

Woods, P. (1999) *Successful Writing for Qualitative Researchers*. London: Routledge.

Woods, P. and Sikes, P. (1987) The use of teacher biographies in professional self-development, in F. Todd (ed.) *Planning Continuing Professional Development*, pp. 161–80. London: Croom Helm.

Woolf, V. (1992) Mr Bennett and Mrs Brown, in V. Woolf and R. Bowlby (ed.) *A Woman's Essays*. London: Penguin.

Zorbaugh, H. (1929) *The Gold Coast and the Slum: A Sociological Study of Chicago's North Side*. Chicago: University of Chicago Press.

| Index

TELLING WOMEN'S LIVES
NARRATIVE INQUIRIES IN THE HISTORY OF WOMEN'S EDUCATION

Kathleen Weiler and Sue Middleton (eds)

This collection brings together the work of scholars exploring the history of women in education in a number of different national settings. The contributors include both established scholars who have completed major studies and younger scholars exploring new directions. All of these writers share an engagement in reflection on the process of history writing and consider the impact of recent theoretical debates on their own scholarship. Their work reflects the influence of feminist theory and poststructuralism, but also of postcolonial theory and theories of the educational state. In these essays, writers address such key issues as the nature of historical evidence, the continuing need to uncover the 'hidden histories' of women as teachers, the ways life history narratives can illuminate women's own conceptions of themselves as women and teachers, the material conditions of teaching as work for women, and the way conceptions of gender have shaped women's experiences in relation to the educational state, the family, class, sexuality and race. These feminist writers also explore the ways they are implicated in the very subject of their research – the educated woman who is also an educator.

Contents
Introduction – Part I: Reflections on memory and historical truth – Teachers, memory and oral history – Workers, professionals, pilgrims: tracing Canadian women teachers' histories – Reflections on writing a history of women teachers – Connecting pieces: finding the indigenous presence in the history of women's education – Part II: Narrative inquiries – Disciplining the teaching body 1968–78: progressive education and feminism in New Zealand – 'To cook dinners with love in them'? Sexuality, marital status and women teachers in England and Wales, 1920–39 – Pathways and subjectivities of Portuguese women teachers through life histories – 'To do the next needed thing': Jeanes teachers in the Southern United States 1908–34 – Where Haley stood: Margaret Haley, teachers' work, and the problem of teacher identity – Index.

176pp   0 335 20173 3 (Paperback)   0 335 20174 1 (Hardback)

TEACHERS' STORIES

David Thomas (ed.)

In *Teachers' Stories* David Thomas and his contributors present an argument for the content and process of teacher training to be enriched by the inclusion of educational biography, both general (grounded Life Histories) and subject specific accounts, as significant ingredients to be stirred in with more formal theoretical and practical aspects of training. Creating educational biographies is one way of introducing students to critical reflection on their 'taken-for-granted' educational beliefs and values, and their origins.

Though not a training manual, *Teachers' Stories* will be of interest to all teacher trainers including the new cohort of trainers – the teacher mentors. Students will also find support for their attempts to introduce, through journals, diaries or logs, their individual experiences as alternative voices to the pre-eminent discourses of the training institution. It is suggested that such opportunities are especially valuable for students and tutors where the student's background and culture provide unusually distinctive experiences with possibilities for course enrichment as well as personal development.

Contents
Introduction – Treasonable or trustworthy text: Reflections on teacher narrative studies – My language experience – The pupil experience: A view from both sides – An education biography and commentary – What do I do next? – Autobiography, feminism and the practice of action research – Making the private public – Crossing borders for professional development: Narratives of exchange teachers – Breaking tadition: The experiences of an alternative teacher in rural school – Empirical authors, liminal texts and model readers – Keys to the past – and to the future – 'Composing a life': Women's stories of their careers – Index.

Contributors
Kath Aspinwall, Waltraud Boxall, Arda L. Cole, Florence Gersten, Morwenna Griffiths, Mary Jean Ronan Herzog, J. Gary Knowles, Doreen Littlewood, Anne Murray, Jennifer Nias, David Thomas, Elizabeth Thomas, Peter J. Woods.

240pp   0 335 19254 8 (Paperback)   0 335 19255 6 (Hardback)

SUBJECT TO FICTION
WOMEN TEACHERS' LIFE HISTORY NARRATIVES AND THE CULTURAL POLITICS OF RESISTANCE

Petra Munro

Petra Munro's *Subject to Fiction* traverses personal and political domains in fascinating and generative ways. Her analysis is grounded in a series of beautifully organized portrayals which then raise a series of questions about intersubjective processes and the very basis of much of existing collaborative and reflexive research.

> Ivor Goodson, Professor, Warner Graduate School of Education,
> University of Rochester, and Professor of Education,
> University of East Anglia

Petra Munro's lively narratives of three American women social studies teachers make an important contribution to the representation of women educators. These narratives account for teachers' lives in ways that previous theories have not. Agency and resistance, power and change, political and occupational identity all figure as compelling themes in these life histories.

> Sari Biklen, Professor in Cultural Foundations of Education
> and Women's Studies at Syracuse University

- How do the life histories of women teachers illuminate the gendered nature of the teaching profession?
- How do women teachers negotiate their own sense of self against/within cultural stereotypes of teachers?

Situated within current feminist/poststucturalist theories regarding the 'subject', this book takes seriously the lives of women teachers. Drawing on the life histories of three teachers, it explores their narrative strategies to author themselves as active agents within and against the essentializing discourses of teaching. The complex and contradictory ways in which these women construct themselves as subjects, while simultaneously disrupting the notion of a unitary subject, provide new ways to think about subjectivity, resistance, power and agency. The implications of this reconceptualization for feminist theorizing, curriculum theory and life history research are woven throughout the book.

Contents

Introduction: impossible fictions – The life of theory – Agnes: 'it is not what you teach, but who you are' – Cleo: 'I could have lived another life and been just as happy' – Bonnie: 'being a teacher is like being a fish out of water' – Rewriting the life – Epilogue – References – Index.

176pp   0 335 20078 8 (Paperback)   0 335 20079 6 (Hardback)